The

PLEASURE OF GARDENING

DESIGNING THE SMALL GARDEN

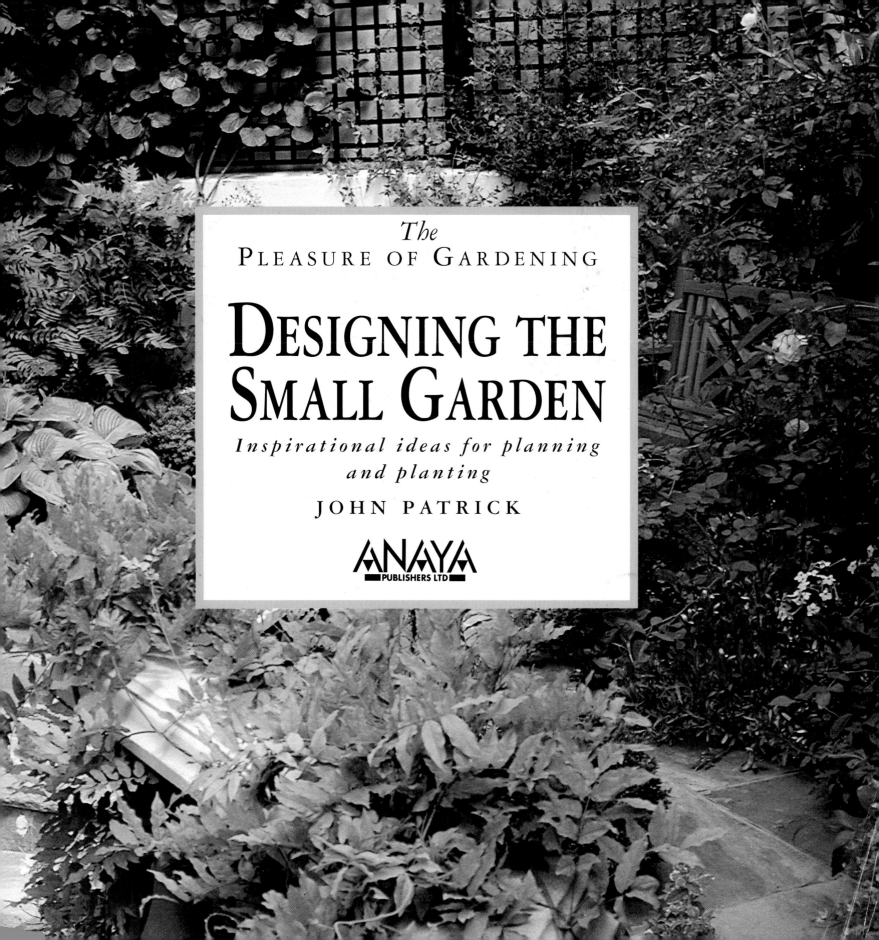

The
PLEASURE OF GARDENING

DESIGNING THE SMALL GARDEN

Inspirational ideas for planning and planting

JOHN PATRICK

ANAYA
PUBLISHERS LTD

CONTENTS

Introduction

Growing up in the country, I was used to space. My gardening was large scale, with drifts of bulbs covering the ground below gnarled damson plums, fruit trees gathered together as orchards, grass mown to different heights, and a meadow lawn — sufficiently different from the rigid geometric rows of the traditional village gardeners for them to question my sanity.

Moving to the city has altered my garden focus. Where once I experimented with plants and could hide the less successful or seasonally unexciting in out-of-the-way corners, I now grow only those I feel confident will contribute. I have learned that there is a very special joy attached to gardening in confined spaces, for now every square inch counts. Furthermore, I can manicure my garden so it looks just so — a contrast indeed to my early wildness, but a wonderful foothold on the real world, an opportunity to nurture, to care and to find immense satisfaction and calmness, away from traffic and from people.

While my small garden territory offers me privacy and seclusion, it also offers me an opportunity to share with others — my growing family, for whom it provides just sufficient adventure, and my friends, for whom it is an extension of my home and myself, a delightful living space beyond the house where we eat and talk and drink in a relaxed way that is impossible within the confines of walls. Here our confines are the sky, the foliage-clad fences, and paving — all a link with nature.

THE SMALL GARDEN IN HISTORY

In this approach to my city garden I am not alone, for town dwellers of all times have enjoyed their gardens. They have enjoyed their garden microclimates, as did the early Egyptians, for whom shade, coolness, a reduction of the play of dusty winds and protection from intruders, both animal and human, played a most important part. While our urban lives are generally safer these days, the town garden remains a haven to which we can retire.

The Romans, too, delighted in their urban retreats. The gardens of Pompeii, unearthed from beneath the ashes spewed forth by Vesuvius, reveal a classic treatment of small urban spaces. Water was important, as was the use of the *trompe l'oeil,* the painted wall designed to make the viewers believe they were looking to the sky, to the buildings beyond, or even to mountains and distant trees.

In medieval Europe, protected town gardens could be highly ambitious and ornamental, the settings for clipped plants and sometimes for precious plants newly introduced from abroad. Some gardens were highly patterned and productive, those of pharmacists being especially notable for the production of the medicinal herbs so vital to the community's well-being. The residents in these towns and cities had the countryside close at hand. This may still be seen in many places today where the fields seem to lie at the very foot of the walls of the city.

The industrial changes of the 19th century and the increased population of the 20th century have seen a change in many of our cities and towns. They are now larger, so that in some the countryside is remote, though our urban parks and gardens still permit strolling, and our mobility results in some people leaving the city for the countryside with remarkable frequency.

Our smaller gardens in particular are remarkably precious. Certainly they were so to the workers of industrial Britain in the last century, for these people took to cultivating specific plant groups to the most remarkable degree of perfection, competing with others in the area to grow the most perfect example of the hyacinth, tulip, ranunculus, anemone, auricula, carnation, pink and polyanthus, and later adding to this list the picotee, sweet william and pansy. What a remarkable contrast it must have been for the worker — from the drudgery of industry to the care and delicacy involved in flower growing.

OPPOSITE: By combining perennials with shrubs and climbers an effective planting scheme of colour, form and texture can be achieved even in a small garden. Seen from above such planting schemes have the quality of a tapestry.

A VARIETY OF OPPORTUNITIES

Today small gardens give the same release, yet the character of the small garden varies as much as towns and cities in different countries. Small gardens may be little more than tiny balcony or roof gardens, in themselves capable of providing a delightful retreat from centrally heated accommodation, or they may be in a courtyard surrounded by high walls, acting as little more, in fact, than an extension to a room, but sufficient to become a vital oasis, given enough imagination.

The owner of a home with even tiny front and rear gardens is extremely fortunate, whether or not there is a side strip as well. The area available permits an extended range of gardening techniques to be used, while with imagination such spaces can be made effectively larger by being subdivided to offer a succession of usable areas to be explored. In this book I shall consider small gardens to be those of ⅛ acre (0.05 hectares) or less.

It is worthwhile differentiating between a small garden and a courtyard. Courtyards suggest enclosure, usually by surrounding walls or another enclosing element. Indeed, a courtyard may be within a building, a focus of the rooms in the building, whereas a small garden, though usually enclosed by a fence, is generally larger and with quite different proportions. I see a courtyard as a special type of small garden.

I enjoy designing small gardens better than any others. They offer the most exciting and challenging projects, for you want to make the most of them. Furthermore, you are completely in control. The effect of every piece of paving, every plant, every inch of garden is vital. In small spaces you can afford to be excitingly detailed,

controlling every effect you achieve in a way that is never quite possible in the larger garden. True, there is no opportunity to create large wild gardens or orchards in your small space, but your ingenuity can allow you to incorporate the elements of these design ideas.

This control allows you to create your small garden so it is exactly as you want it, though you must take care. Avoid trying to grow everything, or displaying every gardening trick you know. Rather, follow one or two themes— you are, after all, creating an overture, not a full-blown symphony. Visit other gardens or read books and magazines to enjoy those themes you miss in your own garden. While this may frustrate you, do realize that a garden is never static. You can always change it, just as you may constantly change your wardrobe or your tastes. Indeed, your needs are also bound to change, and this could cause a wholesale rethink of your garden.

See your small garden as an extension to your house and your lifestyle. Such an extension may be a visual one, or a functional one. The best gardens give you both possibilities. Being able to look from the house into a garden keeps us closer to a world that could otherwise become more and more remote. Even in winter the view of a garden can be soothing. The ability to enjoy the changing seasons is a rich one indeed. Plant a structured plant like a winter hazel (*Corylopsis*) close to your french window so that you can view the garden through it and enjoy its winter bloom. Better still, plant a strongly perfumed spring flowerer such as a *Daphne odora* close to a window so you can enjoy its heady scent on those first warm spring days.

The warmth of these days will draw even the most indolent outside, and this effect will become more frequent as summer draws on. Long, warm evenings cry out for us to extend our living into the garden, and to enjoy an outdoor meal with friends. Children, too, love eating outdoors, but the garden is also for their play, and if you have a family, your small garden must be designed to accommodate the inevitable knocks.

As I hope it is becoming apparent, the small garden is a place of opportunity where much can be achieved. Look at images in this and other books, visit gardens and begin to plan. Your earliest plans may appear as wild schemes in your mind — mine do — but gradually they will become clearer and firmer.

PLANNING YOUR GARDEN

It is critical that you commit your ideas to paper by preparing a plan. Rarely is the first plan entirely satisfactory; refinement and a clearer picture of your goal will result in changes, but piece by piece a satisfactory design will emerge. Just how vital careful planning is will only be appreciated when you come to pay for construction, or to do the work yourself, for the one process is so costly and the other so time-consuming that you cannot afford to make mistakes. You may still make mistakes with planting, but by and large this can be corrected and will not cost you a lot, beyond your pride and a season or two of growth. Get your paving, wall-building, pond-making, or pergola construction wrong, however, and you will have made an expensive mistake. A moment or two of thought at the beginning may save a lot of waste.

ABOVE: White trumpet-shaped flowers of lilies, daturas, and petunias are refreshing in this lush small garden. Recycled brick and stone and painted terracotta pots provide an individual character and visual warmth.

ASSESSING YOUR GARDEN SPACE

Making a plan

The most exciting aspect of designing a garden is that no two gardens are alike. Similar as your site might appear to the one next door, it is not the same. Furthermore, while your likes and dislikes, your values and expectations might largely reflect those of the people next door, the fact is that you will have different needs from your garden. And your garden will become more and more different as you design it, more distinctive, a growing reflection of yourself and the qualities of your site.

Creating gardens begins with the preparation of a good design, and a good design stems from successfully identifying and evaluating the clues provided by your site. I suggest you plot information about your garden on a sheet of graph paper at a scale of 1:100 (1 inch on your plan would be equal

PREVIOUS PAGE: Solid blocks of clipped box offer a wonderful foil to loose plantings especially to the delightfully loose growth of Euphorbia wulfenii.

OPPOSITE: Placement of a central pond makes much of the space of a small garden unusable; however, in this garden there is sufficient space for seating and a table in the corner. The use of paving instead of a lawn reduces maintenance and gives a hard-wearing surface.

to 100 inches of ground, or 1cm to 1 metre). This is an ideal scale for basic planning.

Begin by measuring your site. Measure its boundaries and draw them, noting changes in fencing material, for example where a wall gives way to palings. Give the location of gates, and include your house, its doors and windows in the plan; pay special attention to walls without any windows, because you can put unsightly things like compost bins or clotheslines along these walls. Plot both front and back gardens.

The perimeter of your property marks the area you can have a direct effect on — that is, you can plant and pave according to your plan within your property, whereas beyond this you have little control. You can "borrow" bits, though, in the classic manner of the 18th century English landscape gardeners. The fruit trees next door could provide a backdrop to your garden, or an adjoining park or overhanging street tree could be a lovely feature for your garden. It is worthwhile talking to the people next door; you may be able to agree to plant complementary trees to augment each other's gardens. This is not always possible, but when it works it is invaluable for your garden.

I believe it is vital to plot the features of the landscape, both good and bad, around your garden. Important as the views from the house may be, never forget those from within the garden or views from houses next door, for adjacent windows may overlook the garden sitting area. Creating privacy will be a vital aspect of your design. Your plan could show the areas requiring screening, and those where opportunities exist to borrow. Bear in mind that your own home may not be entirely attractive. The use of paint or a simple climber treatment against a disfigured wall can always achieve great results. Note on your plan where this needs to happen.

FEATURES OF YOUR HOME

The house is the focus to nearly every garden. Through its materials, paint hues, style and period, your house dictates the type of garden you will create. Do not mix architectural styles and periods, and avoid following fashions if you can. Rather design in response to the style of your house, reinforcing its qualities. Cottage gardens work best in front of cottages, though you can be rather more ambitious in a rear yard where your garden is less subject to public scrutiny. The style here may be less a response to the style of your house and more a response to your lifestyle — your garden may well be filled with vegetables and fruit trees here, if that is what interests you.

Analyze your house for details you can build on. You may find an attractive architectural detail, a pattern in brickwork, unusual spacing in windows and doors, an interesting angle of a wall or paving material—each will allow a link between

ABOVE: This long narrow plot has been visually divided into separate spaces by the clever use of paving and planting.

garden and house, and may link indoors with outdoors. Most gardens in modern sub-divisions are rectangular, and such land can be worked with imaginatively, but other plot shapes can also be attractive. Just as your house dictates much of the answer, so too your plot shape can have a most significant effect upon a design. Long narrow plots cry out for division into a series of spaces, L-shaped gardens might be divided into two gardens, one in each limb, and long, narrow strips beside a house can look like tunnels and require care and thought to overcome this problem. Do try to break up the long unbroken space here. For example, the use of simple leafy bowers and climbers to divide the space may assist in breaking the paving line to reduce its linear quality.

ORIENTATION OF THE GARDEN

Your opportunities depend largely upon the orientation of your plot. Eastern morning sun can be a delight; it can allow you to eat outside, encouraging you to venture out on those delightful spring mornings, whereas western sun offers evening opportunity. If your bedroom opens onto the west, you could create a small courtyard where you might sit in the evening enjoying the last warmth of the day. Build upon the mood of a bedroom with softly textured plants in subdued hues, for example, use silvery foliage, and perhaps a delicate fountain.

Orientation to north or south makes an enormous difference—one may make your garden sunny and warm, the other may make it shaded and cool. Make the most of the sun in your garden. Take note of the approximate shadow positions in summer and winter, for they will vary markedly.

Planting will be dictated by sun and shade, as will much of your enjoyment of the garden. If your back garden is especially shaded you may attempt to develop a sunny front garden area, though some privacy is likely to be desirable and you may need to consider how this could conflict with your streetscape and the appearance of your home. A protective screen of walling or a wooden lattice may be a possibility here, but do ensure that you do not need to obtain a planning permit from your local authority. Others living in your street may not appreciate any dramatic change to the visual quality of your streetscape.

Orientation is not just about sun and shade, but also about exposure to wind and rain. Note your dominant winds. If you are exposed you may need to develop a wind-break. A small coastal garden is likely to suffer buffeting winds bearing salt, and you may have to decide upon a compromise between views and weather protection. Rainfall is less significant — you can always stay inside, though it may influence your garden by the creation of rain shadows (areas where little rain falls) and wetter areas, where water moves because of ground shape or because it bounces off walls.

In general there is little you can do to modify the broad climate of your garden — unless you build a conservatory or a glasshouse — but you can create what we call microclimates, small-scale areas where the prevailing climate is modified. In a small garden this is especially important if you wish to sit outside, because you will only be tempted out if conditions are conducive. For example, a pergola with climbers creates shade where once there was sun, and the use of shrubs on the windward side will improve the effect of winds. If you live in the city,

*ABOVE: Clever combinations of containers and surrounding plantings can achieve magical effects if carefully calculated. The verdigris of an old copper is the perfect foil for the buttercup yellow of Welsh poppy (*Mecanopsis cambrica*).*

there are some climatic variations that inevitably occur. For example, temperatures are always higher because of the fuel we burn, the quick runoff of rainfall and the heat-bank of our buildings, while slopes facing the sun are considerably warmer than those sloping away from it.

If your city garden slopes towards the sun you may grow slightly more exotic plants than your rural friends whose plot of land slopes from the sun or is in a shaded valley. Enjoy such opportunities, for they can give your garden personality and style.

THE SOIL IN YOUR GARDEN

Few garden owners enjoy a garden without plants, yet there are designers who create gardens of plastics and minerals and very attractive they may be, though lifeless. Most owners choose to grow plants, however, and then soil becomes a major concern. Soil is below your garden space rather than in it, yet it is vital because of the effect it has on the decorative plants you grow.

With soil, much depends upon where you live. Small country gardens may have enjoyed the benefits of years of organic manure, which can provide excellent soils. In new developments in towns, good soil may have been stripped, to be replaced by a poor alternative, often lacking in nutrients and organic matter. Town soils may also contain years of accumulated rubbish, and you may find buried debris, such as bottles or bricks. Clean these out before planting.

Two vital aspects of your soil need to concern you — its structure, which dictates the balance between air and water, and thus how well plants will grow, and its pH, or level of acidity and alkalinity, which has a significant bearing upon the availability of nutrients and hence the type of plants you can grow. It is also important to check that you do not have compacted soil in areas where you want to plant. This impedes drainage and root growth and can be a threat to the stability of trees if their roots do not manage to penetrate it. Always break up areas of compacted soil.

Test your soil at your local nursery. Add organic material, either your own compost, or manures (be careful not to import weed seeds that pass through the gut of animals), or the by-product of local agriculture if you can get it, for example pea-straw. Otherwise, grow your own green manure of lupins, broad beans or potatoes to improve your soil condition. This also allows you to get the soil clean by controlling weeds in your crop, and is a useful thing to do while you are concentrating on repairing and painting your house rather than on your garden. I do not believe you can do a great deal to achieve long-term, major change to pH. I would prefer to choose plants that enjoy the soil conditions I have — there are always plants to choose from.

THE PLANTS ALREADY GROWING

Unless you have a completely new piece of land, there will always be existing features for you to evaluate and either to retain or to remove, depending upon your assessment of their quality. Among these will be existing plants. Trees are the largest of these, and the most telling. They may be too large, or potentially too large, located in the wrong place, or diseased. In contrast, however, they may also create delightful shade, screen an unsightly view, or offer flower, bark, fruits and fall (autumn) hues so suitable that you could not have made a better choice yourself. The decision to retain or remove the tree will not be difficult in this case, though more often than not the situation will be less clear-cut. Find out as much as you can about your tree before making your final decision. If you are in doubt about keeping the tree it is probably time to remove it — but remember that some local authorities have ordinances on trees to protect them.

Many young trees and shrubs can be moved quite easily, with a few precautions to encourage their survival, but shrubs and perennials generally mature faster than trees, so you may do better to remove these and start afresh unless they are especially attractive. At least make sure that you divide your perennials and retain good, sturdy plants for your new garden. Also make sure you control the weeds on your site. There is nothing worse than discovering pernicious weeds that have survived your redevelopment. These can "hide" among the roots of existing plants,

ABOVE: An ageing tree, like this apple, full of character and charm, can contribute a remarkable maturity to any small garden.

so thorough weeding is essential. Mark the plants you want to keep on your plan, and note their shadow patterns and the spread of trees and shrubs. If your plan includes digging trenches close to the trees, you will damage their roots, and this can have a significant effect on their health and, if serious damage occurs, possibly on their stability as well. Roots are generally quite shallow, so even the implementation of an irrigation system can cause damage. Be careful — hand dig, and avoid breaking roots of 1in (2.5cm) or more.

OLD TREASURES ON YOUR SITE

Vegetation is not the only useful material on a site. You may have good paving that needs re-laying, or a brick shed that could supply attractive old bricks. I recall that an old wash-house provided a most beautiful copper for a garden. With imagination, you can recycle numerous materials. Even old paint cans can make excellent wall containers for plants, if used with flair and splashed with the right shades. Look around in local and country junk shops for charming period gates and bowers to suit your site.

And finally, though it is not part of the site, write down a list of your needs on your plan. A garden is for all the family, so try to ensure that what you want to achieve will meet everybody's needs. This may mean that one or two of your cherished dreams have to be omitted, but the challenge of accommodating other requirements will engage your mind anew and test your imagination to the full. Designing your garden is fun, and you will get inspiration at every turn. I often think of ideas while sitting in traffic, and I never count sheep. Why should I, when there is a garden problem to be solved?

ABOVE: Features of charm and interest add personality to a garden though large urns of this type are inevitably the focus of a small garden because they are so dominant.

GARDEN STYLES

The roomed garden

There is little opportunity to create rooms in the smallest of gardens; a seat beneath a tree may have to suffice for a separate room. However, in a larger garden, dividing up the overall space into a series of smaller gardens may be quite attractive. Though it may seem perverse, this can achieve a sense of increased space. Dividing the garden has other advantages as well: it will allow you to explore different options for using the garden, just as you might have different use options in your house, where different rooms support different activities.

In your home you decorate rooms to support your activities. (As a boy I painted my bedroom pillar-box red and black, though quite what activity this was designed to support, apart from my assertion of my independence, I am unsure.) Similarly, different planting schemes can support different purposes of a garden space, as the plants you choose will create different moods.

Dividing a garden into rooms has a further advantage in that it can create more comfortably proportioned spaces. Rather than having to deal with a single long space, you may find it possible to form a series of linked spaces, each of attractive proportions. The simplest solution would be to divide a long, rectangular block into a series of approximate squares, and this solution can work well. But when the relationship of width to length changes this simple solution may become less suitable.

Importantly, the "rooms" created should relate to each other so that there is a sense of continuity and cohesion about them. For example, you may use consistent framing or enclosing elements, such as an enclosing hedge or fence, or a linking paving material. Placing the enclosed spaces on a single vista or viewline can also work.

The opportunities that arise from the creation of rooms in a garden are endless. Trying to overcome conflicts is an important part of design, for example, around a pool you may wish to separate children from adults who are enjoying a relaxing lunch, or players of ballgames from a reading area. Using rooms creates both protection and separation, a vital and sensible step in overcoming conflict situations.

The garden designed addresses several of these issues. The garden is the largest size that I would still call a small garden. By creating a series of rooms, allowance is being made for an area for eating outside, space for sitting outside quietly, and a grassed area for children to play in.

OPPOSITE: In a garden a defined space creates a feeling of a walled room and can be an extension of the living space of the house.

PREVIOUS PAGE: Garden style derives from assembling various features to reinforce an initial concept. This small garden achieves its impact by combining natural stone, formal hedging and loose planting to create a marvellous classical effect.

The roomed garden

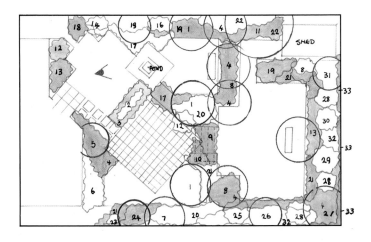

Key to planting

1. *Malus* 'Golden Hornet'
2. *Lavandula angustifolia* 'Hidcote'
3. *Tulbaghia violacea*
4. *Ophiopogon japonicus*
5. *Fatsia japonica*
6. *Helleborus foetidus*
7. *Amelanchier canadensis*
8. *Luma apiculata* (Pruned to maintain tight form)
9. *Rosa* 'Francis E. Lester'
10. *Clematis cirrhosa* 'Balearica'
11. *Sorbus aria* 'Lutescens'
12. *Euphorbia chariacas* ssp. *chariacas*
13. *Geranium renardii*
14. *Rosa* 'Constance Spry'
15. *Buddleia alternifolia* 'Argentea'
16. *Abelia* x *grandiflora*
17. *Gaura lindheimeri*
18. *Sedum spectabile* 'Autumn Joy'
19. *Geranium phaeum*
20. *Iris foetidissima*
21. *Pachysandra terminalis*
22. *Polystichum setiferum*
23. *Viburnum opulus* 'Compactum'
24. *Mahonia* x *media* 'Buckland'
25. *Hydrangea paniculata* 'Grandiflora'
26. *Camellia japonica* 'Materhorn'
27. *Lagerstroemia indica*
28. *Spiraea cantoniensis*
29. *Osmanthus delavayi*
30. *Carpenteria axillaris*
31. *Gordonia axillaris*
32. *Anemone* x *hybrida* 'Prince Henry'
33. *Trachelospermum japonicus*

This design builds upon the angle of the rear wall of the building and does so by using lines at 45° to the axis through the site. This allows planting to encroach into the garden rather than simply lining the fence. The back of the house is likely to shade the area immediately adjacent to the house, so a sitting area, by being pulled away from the house, can obtain more sun. Being central to the garden, the sitting area forms the fulcrum to the design, and sets the position for the play lawn beyond a bower, leading to the end of the garden where a seat will not only provide a focus but a most useful sunny seating spot. The diagonal through the paved square forms a part of the axis to the seat. A simple timber bower frames this viewline from the house. The second diagonal on the paved area leads to a small raised pond with a fountain placed so that it is parallel to the angled portion of the house. A raised pond of this type is a wonderful focus and serves as the linking element for three different garden rooms: a paved area; the enclosed, reflective lawn area, and the simple lawn adjacent to the rear of the house. Having a raised pond means it is possible to sit on the wall and really benefit from the presence of the cooling water. Pavers set in the grass at the base of the wall reinforce the turf, to prevent it being worn out by this use. Similarly, paving outside the back door overcomes problems of wear.

Planting supports all of these objectives, with low planting against the windows of the house, in this case *Helleborus orientalis* and *Ophiopogon japonicus* permitting views into the garden. Trees enclose the quietest part of the garden, a row of three *Malus* 'Golden Hornet' providing a series of frames to the main garden views, while a clipped row of *Luma apiculata* provides a solid enclosure. These effectively divide the garden. Use of the evergreen myrtle ensures that the rear garden shed is screened.

Throughout the garden, planting is designed to provide a combination of seasonal displays, *Clematis cirrhosa* var. *balearica* giving winter flower hues on the bower, to be followed later by the fine *Rosa* 'Francis E. Lester'.

The large paved area also provides decoration for the site. The frame of the paving uses a different material from the in-fill, ensuring not only a contrast in shades, but also a sense of definition to this space. It is sufficiently large for a family to enjoy outside meals. The use of *Lavandula angustifolia* and *Tulbaghia violacea* offers an enclosure to this space and separation from the adjacent lawn.

In general, the aim of this design is to establish a series of spaces and to reduce the sensation of seeing the entire site at a single glance.

A garden for entertaining

The joys of being able to use an outside area for entertaining are considerable. Firstly, there is less formality about eating alfresco, and this is always attractive, especially if on vacation or where children are involved. Entertaining outside also tends to indicate lighter, more easily assembled meals, the use of bright crockery and possibly even bright cushions on seats, a contrasting umbrella and the delicious effects of light and shade, combined with the scent of plants on the air. Who among us could resist such an opportunity?

While in some areas the best time for eating outside is the middle of the day, when the sun is up and shade is needed, in other places the long, drawn-out sunsets encourage the use of the garden on fine balmy evenings. While an umbrella gives an effective roof to a space well into the night, the use of a fountain and a few candles or well-located lights can provide a special quality, encouraging a lingering meal at night.

The potential for using an outdoor eating area is bounded only by your imagination. Extending cocktail parties outside can offer coolness and comfort, while children's parties outdoors can reduce the need to tidy up; after all, using a hose and a broom is simpler than using a vacuum cleaner.

There are some essential features to consider when providing an outdoor entertaining area. Firstly, provide the best contact possible between internal and external spaces, so that the two can effectively relate. At least one set of double opening doors is ideal, and more are desirable if space permits. Surfaces should be smooth, without traps such as wide, low tubs to fall over or sudden changes, such as uneven cobbles. Point up paved surfaces — that is, fill with mortar — or butt joint to ensure that there are no traps for heels.

Outdoor eating areas need to be larger than those for equivalent activities inside, so make sure the paved area provided is adequate for your purposes and ensure that it is not too far from the cooking area to the eating area. A barbecue is ideal. Provide a propane (gas) point in your garden if you think you will need one.

Purchase sensible outdoor furniture. Good teak settings are excellent, but they are very heavy and as a result may not be easy to move. Teak is therefore not a good solution if you live alone. Permanent heavy furniture also precludes using your garden for anything else, which is a problem where the garden is really small. Choose good-quality collapsible furniture that can be put away when not in use. Add bright cushions and matching table napkins, to provide liveliness to your outdoor entertaining.

OPPOSITE: For most city gardeners an outdoor sitting space is vital. Colour in furniture and walls is just as legitimate as that of flowers, and provides a most exciting element in this garden.

A garden for entertaining

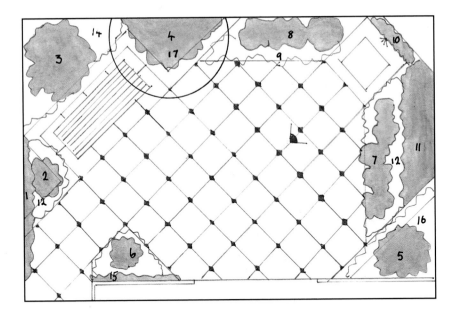

Key to planting

1. *Solanum crispum* 'Glasnevin'
2. *Euphorbia wulfenii*
3. *Choisya ternata*
4. *Robinia pseudoacacia*
5. *Cistus* x *syprius*
6. *Rosmarinus* 'Miss Jessop's Variety'
7. *Ceratostigma willmottianum*
8. *Nandina domestica*
9. *Sedum spectabile*
10. *Hosta plantaginea*
11. *Prunus glandulosa*
12. *Ajuga* 'Jungle Beauty'
13. *Ajuga* 'Jungle Beauty'
14. *Euphorbia robbiae*
15. *Pyracantha* 'Orange Glow'
16. *Campanula portenschlagiana*
17. *Bergenia* 'Silberlicht'

In the site designed, several solutions have been applied to achieve particular effects. This garden is genuinely small, so treatments have allowed the retention of as large an open space as possible to accommodate a table and chairs.

Visually the space has been enlarged by the use of paving on a diagonal line, at 45° to the house and boundary walls. This ensures that the garden appears larger. Once this angle is set the garden features need to respond to it — for example, a pond occupies a corner of the site where it intrudes least on the space but offers an effective focus to the site. Similarly, the seat is placed on an angle at the other side of the site. The site is flat, and there may be an argument for keeping it so, but the use of simple retaining walls permits changes of level to be established while reinforcing the design. This happens in two corners of the site, one used to accommodate the seat and the other to balance the raised pond.

I always believe that small gardens of this type should be decorative, and this includes not only the planting but also the paving. A large square paver might be used, with a second paver as a dropper to establish a contrast, set into the corner of each paving slab. This will increase the cost of the paving because of the cutting involved, but on such a small area this increase is not likely to be significant. Note that droppers are not used at every paver corner — this would be too predictable — but they do provide a central focus to the area and carry through to the pond and wall fountain.

To maximise the usable area of the site, design the doors to the house so that they hinge back as far as possible.

Planting for this garden needs to retain a year-round quality. Inevitably, though flowers are important, foliage and form are likely to be major elements of the design in that they will extend the season of display beyond the flowering periods. It is most important that you can add flowers to this garden for the season when you wish to use the garden. There is little room for pots of plantings, so add bedding plants in discrete areas of the garden, to provide a finishing touch. A bunch of flowers on the table will add interest.

In this proposal, a deciduous tree has been selected to provide summer shade but winter light. *Robinia pseudacacia* may eventually become too large, but it could be removed and replaced when this happens. Some thinning will ensure that it retains an open canopy and an attractive shadow pattern in the summer.

Climbing plants have been used to soften walls at every opportunity, though the *Pyracantha* 'Orange Glow' is a shrub trained against the wall to provide fruit display, while *Solanum crispum* 'Glasnevin' fills a more traditional climber's role on a lattice on the wall. *Euphorbia characias* subsp. *wulfenii,* the *Robinia, Bergenia* and *Ajuga* 'Jungle Beauty' all provide effective textural elements in the composition.

The fountain in the corner of the garden will be shaded, and while it is preferable that it should receive more sun, it will provide a delightful sound that fills the garden.

The romantic garden

Few places conjure up a sense of romance better than a garden. Part of the joy of viewing a late Victorian painting of a cottage is the sense of romance created by elements such as a semi-derelict house, thatched roof, and wild chickens about the hedgerow and roadside. But most romantic of all are the vivid plants climbing the walls of the house and filling every square inch of the garden, so that you can almost smell the perfume lingering on the air in front of the painting. Sadly, not all of these qualities are available to the owner of the small garden today, certainly not in our tidier suburbs anyway!

Yet there are elements of this image that can be used by the home gardener in the city, even with restricted space, particularly the choice of plants. The appeal is in the use of plants to achieve an unrestricted and zestful flamboyance. The edge of the paving is softened by flowing masses of plants, so that the structural qualities achieved by design are softened. Structures themselves, selected primarily to provide an overhead containment, also offer an opportunity for roses to scramble and decorate with their wild abandon, for petals to be shed on the ground, and for the air to be filled with heady perfume.

Such a garden scene requires a consistency of response appropriate with all the elements to the style. Paving should not be sophisticated; perhaps a combination of brick and gravel would be attractive. Picket fences might offer suitable treatment for an enclosure, while a leafy bower could be composed of simple lines rather than reflecting any effort at sophistication. Seats, too, need to have a homeliness rather than a high degree of sophistication. The popular Lutyens timber seat, ideal for the classic formal garden, would be sadly out of place here, and the more polished and formal containers such as terracotta planters would appear incongruous. An old copper or a stone sink would be appropriate.

One of the real problems for the owner of a small garden in creating a romantic garden is that so much of its content has a relatively short-lived display. Many of the plants cherished for their wealth of summer hues are deciduous; my approach would be to use a number of evergreen plants to provide at least some structure for the design in winter.

So many plants add to the delights of roses. Scents are vital, though many of the plants suited to this style of gardening lack scent, and contribute only their lush growth and scintillating flowers. Phlox, campanulas, poppies and irises are vital, and lavenders and perovskias, the little pinks and some clematis would be obligatory. Lilacs and buddleias, too, combine well, and for those sensitive to effective plant combinations, the opportunity to use the mauves of old-fashioned roses, lilacs, onions, armeria and purple-leaved sages is irresistible.

One word of warning about these gardens. For all their apparently simple style, they require considerable maintenance. The greater the diversity of planting that is achieved in a garden, the greater the knowledge and maintenance required to ensure the long-term well-being of the garden. A garden of this type is not one for anyone who requires a low-maintenance garden. However, for those who love the sense of tradition in the garden, a romantic garden has much to offer.

OPPOSITE: Flowing masses of plants evoke the atmosphere of the romantic garden, especially heritage roses and species with fragrant flowers or foliage.

The romantic garden

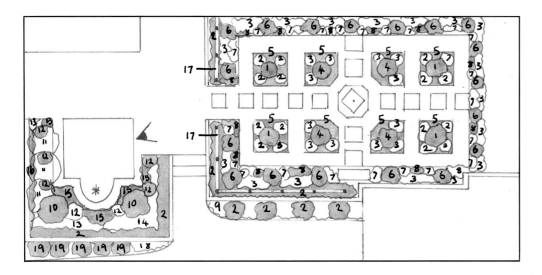

Key to planting

1. *Rosa* 'Mary Rose'
2. *Lavandula angustifolia*
3. *Gaura lindheimeri*
4. *Rosa* 'Duchesse d'Angouleme'
5. *Nepeta* x *mussimi*
6. *Dierama pulcherrimum*
7. *Agapanthus* 'Baby Blue'
8. *Geranium endressii* 'Wargraves Pink'
9. *Brachycome multifida*
10. *Rosa chaucer*
11. *Camellia sasanqua*
12. *Iris germanica*
13. *Anemone japonica* 'Alba'
14. *Lychnis coronaria* 'Alba'
15. *Bergenia cordifolia*
16. *Ficus pumila*
17. *Clematis* 'Ernest Markham'
    and *Rosa ophelia* (alternating)
18. *Ajuga* 'Jungle Beauty'
19. *Agapanthus orientalis*

In the illustrated plan, roses make a major contribution to the design. No other plant is associated with romance to the same degree, a fact that is hardly surprising given not only the quality of the rose flower and its fragrance, but also its history and origins.

Significantly, most of the roses selected are recurrent, a vital feature of roses selected for smaller gardens where the repetition adds to the sense of space. Those that are not recurrent would be chosen for outstanding qualities — for example, the delightful pink-flowered 'Mme Gregoire Staechlin' is selected for its breathtaking, slightly pendulous creamy pink flowers. Others, for example *Rosa* 'Geranium', is grown for its splendid flowers, single and bright, but also for its generous orange-red hips.

In this plan, paths link spaces which are separated by an open timber frame. Vigorous roses cover this frame while a fountain is the focus to the enclosed garden. Terracotta stepping stones indicate the path line and are an attractive contrast to the pea gravel of the greater part of the garden.

Romance is provided by the massed roses in beds dropped into the gravel in a pattern. The roses are 'Chaucer' and 'Iceberg' augmented by massed herbaceous plantings of *Geranium endressii, Gaura lindheimeri, Tulbaghia violacea, Agapanthus* 'Baby Blue' and *Sedum spectabile.* Lavenders provide an edge to the garden, their scent offering a most important feature.

This type of garden could be augmented by pretty seats or perhaps a dovecot, out of place in many gardens, but adding a touch of romance to this one.

The private garden

Small gardens in cities are a feature of modern life. In many towns and cities, gardens have never been large, though the 19th century onward saw a sudden expansion in cities, so that suburbs with large homes in sizeable gardens became popular for the middle class. Suburbs with houses set in gardens grew, offering a new quality of life for those commuting to work in the city. Today these suburbs are being consolidated, either by the construction of other buildings in the gardens, or by demolition of houses and construction of new homes with smaller gardens.

Now the problem is creating an effective garden in a smaller space and ensuring privacy so that you can enjoy it and relax to the full. Often your garden will not be totally private, but it is reassuring to feel that at least you are not always overlooked.

Another aspect of privacy is the need to lessen outside noise. Problems that arise from adjoining houses include loud radios, the cries of children, and garrulous people. This problem is not easily addressed, and is not overcome by planting. Unless you can use the plants in great density, planting will have a negligible effect on noise levels, but there will be a psychological benefit from

OPPOSITE: Use of massed, loose shrubs and perennials provides softness in a garden and achieves a romantic effect, a perfect foil to the harshness of city streets.

not seeing the source of the noise. Walls have more effect in cutting down noise, but are expensive and may not suit the setting. Disguising the noise may be the best option — wind chimes or fountains may help — though you can do little to overcome the wailings of the latest sensation on compact disk.

Visual privacy is a priority; this gives you confidence that your garden is available for your pleasure. Privacy is achieved by blocking inward views, and it may be that to achieve this you have to create a completely encircling mass of planting, creating a garden fortress, impenetrable to all except those with a machete. This may suit some, notably those with a penchant for large-growing, lush, jungle-like plants; however, for most of us privacy needs to be tempered by access to light and the opportunity to use the bulk of the garden for purposes other than planting. It is important, when developing privacy, to establish the source of the views. If you are concerned only about intrusions of nosy characters who look over the top of your fence, then simply raising the level by using lattice and climbers may be sufficient, and will leave you with the opportunity to enjoy sun over much of your site for most of the year.

But establishing privacy is usually more complex than this. In many instances the invasive eye is at a higher level, looking down onto the garden. A single window

that allows for prying is generally not difficult to screen — a tree planted between the window and your patio will eventually achieve an effect once it has grown. If more windows intrude, the problem is greater, and you could end up with a wall of trees. Instead of planting such trees in a row, do break them up, if space permits, to create a structured approach to your screen. This will give the planting a three-dimensional effect.

Remember that as you move through the garden your degree of privacy will vary. Where one area is private, another may be open, and this may suit you quite well: though some of the garden may be exposed you can be secure in the knowledge that other areas are totally visually private, and use these accordingly, for example for eating outside.

Privacy is not only about being overlooked, but is also about being able to see adjoining houses, sheds, and so on. Good screening planting can contribute to privacy in terms of being overlooked, and to a sense of security by shielding adjacent structures. Remember that the closer you are to a screening tree, for example, the greater the area it will visually screen, while the closer the tree is to the source of your concern the more broadly effective it will be. It is not difficult to work out the best location for a screening plant if you move about your garden and gauge the impact of your proposed tree.

The private garden

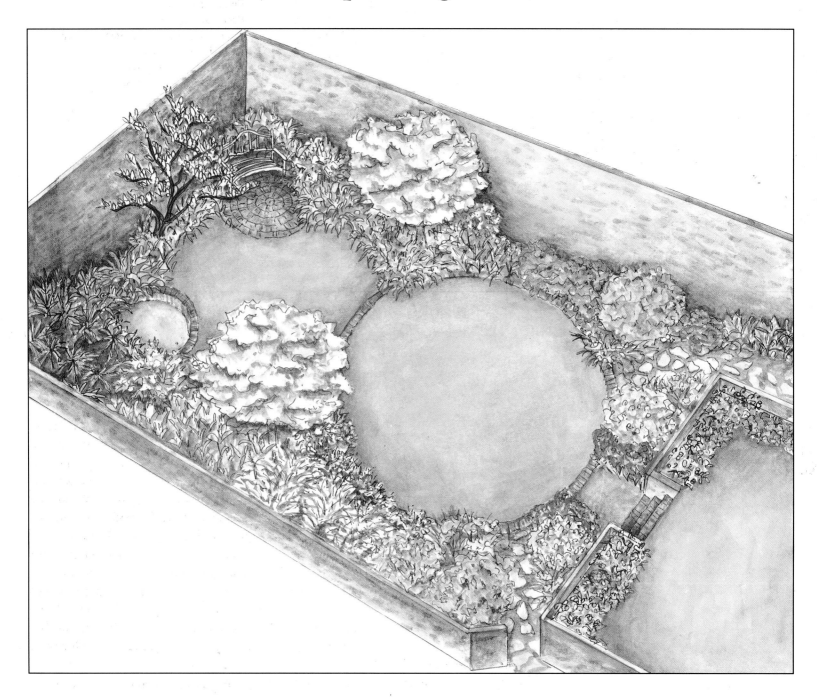

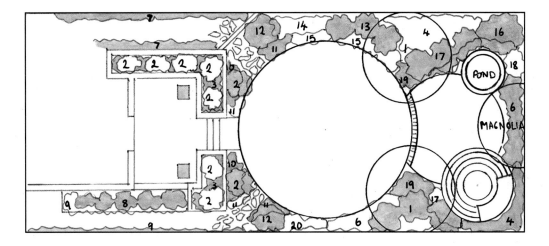

Key to planting

1. *Prunus* 'Shirotae'
2. *Rosa* 'Chaucer'
3. *Geranium endressii* interplanted with *Tulbachia violacea*
4. *Hedychium gardnerianum*
5. *Trachelopsermum jasminoides*
6. *Iris fimbriata*
7. *Bergenia* x *schmidtii*
8. *Nandina domestica*
9. *Iris unguicularis*
10. *Lychnis coronaria*
11. *Tulbaghia violacea*
12. *Syringa* x *persica*
13. *Spiraea* x *arguta*
14. *Prunus tenella* 'Firehill'
15. *Heuchera micrantha* 'Palace Purple'
16. *Mahonia lomariifolia*
17. *Hydrangea quercifolia*
18. *Hosta plantaginea*
19. *Dicentra formosa* 'Alba'
20. *Sedum spectabile* 'Autumnale'

In the design illustrated, the garden has been broken into different zones to achieve varying degrees of privacy. There are two-level houses all around the site, each of them with a small garden of similar size to the one in the plan. Total privacy for the garden could only be secured by extensive planting all around the garden, something that is not desirable, and would remove most of the light from the garden.

The creation of zones is in part a response to this situation. Firstly, a paved area is created close to the house, where an overhead canopy and some restricted side planting create sufficient enclosure to offer a sense of comfort for outdoor eating. Secondly, there is a large circular lawn on a lower level, edged by brick and entered not only from the terrace via steps but also from either side of the house. Finally, there is a lower lawn, circular and separated by a step made up of the brick edge to the upper lawn. This lower lawn is given privacy and shade by a canopy of trees, making it a place for plant cultivation and a place to sit and read, removed from the intrusion of adjacent buildings. A circle of brick paving provides a hard stand for a seat.

Gardening in such a place permits the exploitation of these different zones. The terrace is largely sunny and full of varying hues, the site for pots of display planting which includes annuals and roses. The middle lawn is the place for shrubs and herbaceous plants, and the setting for paired trees, the focus to the axial lines of the paths. *Prunus* 'Shirotae' is used in this case, and is sufficiently large to enclose the space of the lower lawn. The focus to the garden is an already existing *Magnolia* x *soulangeana,* giving the garden a very strong burst of spring brightness. In the shade of this garden, massed shade-loving plants give foliage interest and contrasting shades.

The height of fences around the garden is increased by the use of a surrounding lattice, and climbing plants, notably *Trachelospermum jasminoides,* are trained over the lattice to reduce the intrusion of adjacent buildings and to give an effective greenness to the whole garden. Privacy is often best achieved by the creation of a green oasis.

The foliage garden

The joy of foliage is all around us, to be touched and to be viewed both on its own and in conjunction with paved surfaces and walls. The use of foliage for different textures takes a garden into a new dimension, extending its quality from the simple beauty of flowers to a more enduring and more classical approach. Significantly, foliage plants produce flowers too, so that their use does not in any way exclude the presence and effect of flowers. It simply means that by careful selection we have obtained a more extensive decoration. Many foliage plants we would choose would be evergreen too, extending the period of display.

Fundamental to the creation of a foliage garden is the appreciation of the qualities that foliage offers, and in this respect we need to consider the value of greenery and the value of foliage shade. Green is important in the design of gardens: though we may grow plants to provide rich fall (autumn) tints in red, gold, and yellow, and though spring might offer delicate pinks and fierce reds in foliage, for example from *Acer pseudoplatanus* 'Brilliantissimum' or

OPPOSITE: Foliage need not be large to contribute a textured planting scheme. Box balls with small leaves are the perfect foil to the masses of blue-green Hosta sieboldiana *'Elegans', ivy and euphorbia foliage. Note how flower colour contributes little to the effect of this planting scheme.*

Pieris 'Forest Flame', green in its various shades is predominant in our gardens through the year. From the silver grey-greens of lavender, through to the deep lustrous green of *Camellia sasanqua,* from the blue-green of *Acanthus mollis* to the yellow-green of *Philadelphus coronarius,* there is an extraordinary diversity of greens — indeed, sufficient for us to be able to design a garden of greens alone. Add to this the range of foliage in purples, silvers and variegations, and the opportunities created by foliage become readily apparent.

Many of these fine foliage plants also produce perfume, an enjoyable element in its own right. Grasp the leaf of bay or rosemary, or break open the leaf of a eucalypt, to experience the power of foliage scent. Note that it is the leaves of plants from hot, dry environments that produce volatile oils with wonderful smells. Such a foliage garden could be especially suited to a Mediterranean climate garden, where many of these plants prosper.

Much of the quality of a foliage plant depends upon the manner of presentation of the foliage. Branches that are long and elegant and offer foliage for admiration, as in the delightfully leaved *Camellia sasanqua,* or leaves that are finely divided so that they make a strong architectural presence, as in *Mahonia lomariifolia,* one of the great foliage plants, are clearly contenders for inclusion in any foliage garden. Just why I find the leaf of *Camellia*

sasanqua so much more lovely than the generally glossier and plumper leaf of *C. japonica* I am not sure, except that it does seem to me that there is much to be said for neatness where foliage is concerned.

More complex foliage shapes have their attractions, but not if used in a large mass without a few solid, finer foliage plants around. A foliage garden depends upon the effective judgment and assessment of plants, so that they are put together to form a rich and sophisticated picture and not just a random mess. The use and appreciation of foliage plants is a relatively sophisticated subject, not one that attracts those who have just begun to have an interest in plants, for appreciation of foliage depends upon quite subtle qualities.

While a foliage garden may be appreciated from a distance, for example viewed from a window, many of its finer qualities become apparent on closer investigation. Touch is necessary to fully appreciate the hairy leaf of *Salvia argentea,* while the rugose leaf surface of *Rodgersia aesculifolia* is only fully valued when closely inspected, though its shape, strong and magnificent, may be appreciated readily enough.

As foliage has such excellent texture, it becomes inevitable that foliages will be combined with other richly textured elements of a garden. Pavings, containers, furniture — all offer attractive opportunities, as, too, does the surface of water where foliage may be reflected.

The foliage garden

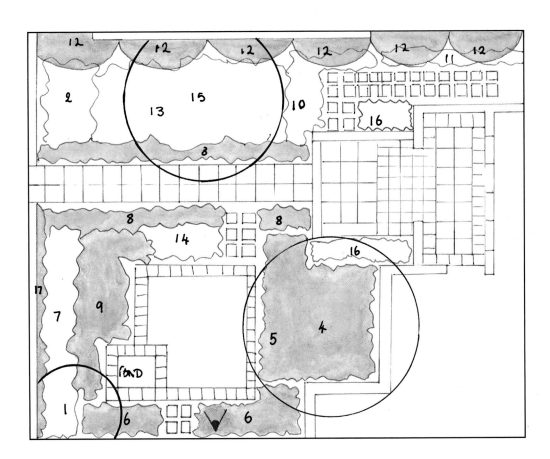

This design is for a small front garden, and uses a combination of foliages and gravels to create a garden of charm and interest. In this case both functional and aesthetic issues have been addressed, while the foliage planting is used to combine with flowers in the creation of a garden in various shades of blue and silver. In general, foliage plants in silvery shades enjoy sunlight, and the garden is designed to be sunny and lively in feel. To build on this, use gravels and terracotta for paving.

Access from the front gate to the house is by means of a terracotta path of large slabs. In front of the steps to the house, this widens out to create a plinth. As is often the case, children passing through the garden are unlikely to use the front gate if an alternative option exists. In this site, access is also available through the driveway gates, so a diagonal path is provided across the site by means of terracotta steppers and a large terracotta-edged, gravel-paved area. The use of a weak concrete mix beneath the gravel will reduce maintenance and ensure that only a thin layer of gravel is needed. Use your local gravel for its tints, and for interest. Adjacent to the gravel is a square pond able to accommodate a fountain.

Planting through this garden is designed to develop a theme of blues and silvery tones, in response to the toning of the house and the presence of the sun. This builds on the Mediterranean character.

Trees such as *Jacaranda mimosifolia* and *Olea europaea* are enhanced by climbers such as the show-stopping, blue-flowered *Thunbergia grandiflora*. The massing of strong foliage plants like *Dietes grandiflora* and *Agapanthus praecox* ssp. *orientalis*, *Perovskia atriplicifolia* and *Helleborus corsicus* helps retain a relatively low-maintenance approach, with a low level of watering, which is eminently suited to this garden's climatic zone. Given the blues and silver tones used throughout this garden, the effect can be extended through to the pond by using glazed tiles of blue, possibly with yellow and white as a contrast to achieve an attractive and effective tie between the planting and pool.

The pattern garden

Pattern gardens take us back to the earliest gardens, when the clipping of plants to form neat hedges was a popular element of garden design. The popularity of patterned gardens has waxed and waned: admired by the great gardeners of Italy and France, they were largely absent from the great landscapes of England.

Today, pattern gardens are recognized as a simple way of achieving a neat and attractive garden with relatively straight-forward maintenance. Given a little thought, they can be both bright and imaginative.

Traditional pattern gardens used clipped foliage plants of contrasting textures and hues, combined frequently with gravels, to create visual interest and beauty. There are many who have adopted this approach and adapted it to their gardens. Others have adopted a more modern strategy, seeing an opportunity to create strong patterns simply by using mass plantings of well-textured plants, such as *Ophiopogon japonicus* or *Hemerocallis fulva*, to create free-flowing patterns. Perhaps the master of this approach has been the great South American designer Roberto Burle Marx, who has created breathtaking results in many gardens with sweeps of bold plants and patterns of bright tiles and pavers.

OPPOSITE: The use of patterned clipped hedges, as a contrast to soft plantings of roses, and gravel as a paving provides a magnificent formal garden. Central height, here provided by a large urn, provides the variation essential to achieve full effect in this style of garden.

Note that such gardens look best when viewed from above, for the patterns become much clearer and more easily interpreted. Houses with upper-floor windows would be well served by a pattern garden, whereas in those with a ground level only the patterns would be far less obvious. This is certainly the case with abstract patterns. Strong geometric patterns can also be enjoyed at ground level.

Pattern need not only stem from planting, but paving can also contribute to this effect. There are now so many paving materials available that pattern can be easily achieved by carefully selecting from among them. Pattern with paving may stem from using a single material, for example brick, in different placements. Such patterns are quiet but stylish, and can achieve subtle effects. Bricks laid end to end increase the sense of distance, good for a relatively short path. Alternatively, laid in a herring-bone pattern, they achieve a dynamic visual effect with a sense of movement. A more neutral pattern would be one such as basket weave.

Always try to relate materials to the style of your garden. Brick may either be very formal, for example if it echoes the use of brick in a large house, or quite informal, as, for example, in front of my own cottage. Introduce terracotta and glazed tiles, and you will achieve a quite different mood — likewise with natural stones in a check pattern of stone and cobbles. In the last instance, though the effect could be very pleasing, such a surface would not be easy to move across. Overcome this problem by

using a pattern of two smooth paving materials, and gradually change to paving and cobbles or paving and planting at the edge. Such treatments can achieve dramatic and very beautiful design effects.

The combination of plants and paving to create pattern is not new. Parterres, knots and even turf mazes all achieve this effect. Where a suitable space is available, a maze of paths in a concentric pattern leading to a sundial or a pond can be most attractive.

Not only low hedges can be used to display patterns from planting — taller-growing plants can be used for this effect as well. The orchard is a particular form of such a garden, with trees planted in grids for simple maintenance. Small gardens do not really permit this theme to be explored on a large scale, but a pattern of trees planted on a regular grid out of a surface of, say, gravel can be visually pleasing from above, and exciting to move through. Such a design could provide a striking low-maintenance treatment for a front garden, especially if combined with a well-chosen seat and a pond.

The creation of diverse spaces between hedges permits a range of treatments to be used. In a small garden there is insufficient space for grass, but gravels of different shades could be used as a contrast to the exuberance of the planting.

Low hedges can be formed from many plants, *Lavandula angustifolia, Santolina chamaecyparissus, Buxus sempervirens* and *B.s.* 'suffruticosa' and even dwarf plants of strong constitution, for example *Armeria maritima*.

The pattern garden

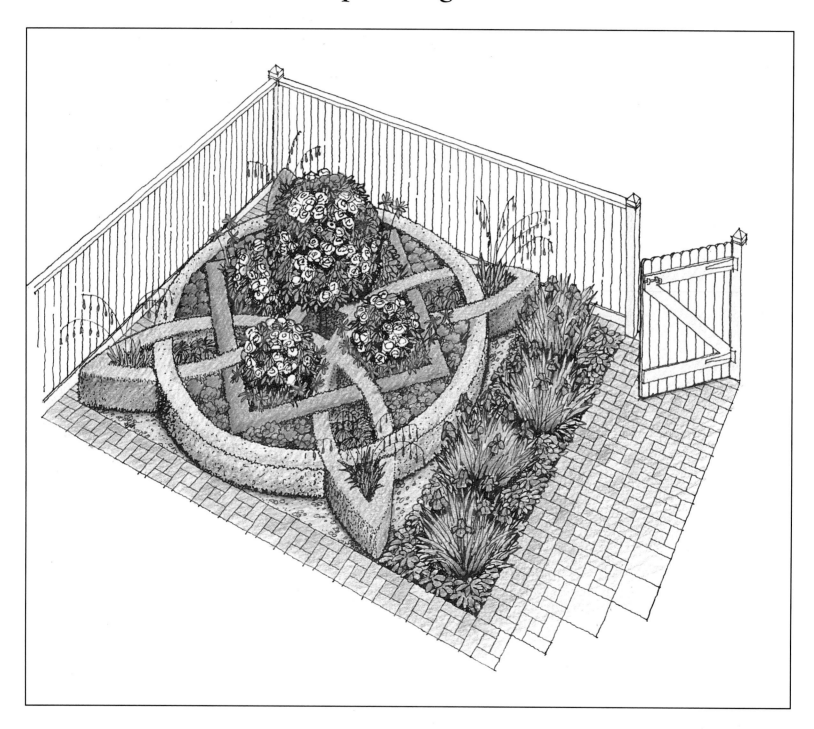

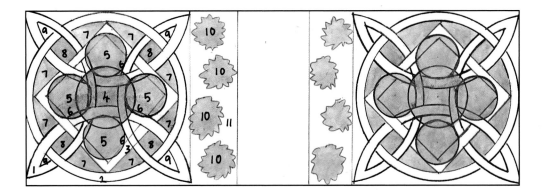

Key to planting

1. *Lavandula angustifolia* (Munstead Lavender or English Lavender)
2. *Buxus sempervirens* 'Suffruticosa' (Dwarf Box)
3. *Rosmarinus officinalis* (Rosemary)
4. *Rosa* 'Iceberg' Standard
5. *Rosa* 'Iceberg' Bush
6. *Gaura lindheimeri* (Gaura)
7. *Armeria maritima* (Sea Pink)
8. *Ophiopogon japonicus* (Mondo Grass)
9. *Dierama pendulum* (Fairies Fishing Rod)
10. *Iris germanica* 'Blackout'
11. *Ajuga* 'Burgundy lace' (Bugle)

In this design, a traditional approach has been used involving the use of low, clipped hedges. In this case the hedges lie either side of a central front path to a small house. This gives a symmetry to the site, which is reflected in the design. However, the design also allows for two strips of bright plantings, one on each side of the path. This could be changed seasonally to offer an effective planting display: tulips with forget-me-nots for spring, pink pelargonium with a mauve verbena and silver *Cinererea maritima* for summer. It is a good idea to follow this tactic of change in a garden that otherwise has a well-developed consistency.

Hedges in this garden form a complex pattern of circles and arcs within a square. A pattern need not be so complex; my own garden consists of two squares inside each other, linked by short central arms, the effect being to achieve four L-shapes around a central square.

I enjoy using a strong framework as a basis for perennial plants, for example a low box hedge to provide a formal structure over which perennials can cascade in summer. In the example here, however, the use of lavender as a major part of the hedging precludes this treatment, as lavenders have an abhorrence of shade, so instead a pretty display of standard and bush roses is combined with lavenders and display plants to achieve a very romantic effect. To my mind this is the great attraction of patterned gardens: they can be stiff and formal, they can be flouncy and full of flowers cascading over hedges, or they can provide the basis for herbs and vegetables. The solution is in your hands, the use of the pattern providing a consistent reference point from which to work.

The terraced garden

Sloping sites offer challenges to all garden designers, though they also offer opportunities. Few gardens are completely flat, and those with slight changes in level provide exciting opportunities for variation and change absent from the flat site. I would advise responding to the quality of your site and achieving changes in levels by means of plants and their variations, rather than with random and meaningless mounds. Such an approach can waste considerable space in a small garden while achieving few real benefits, except perhaps allowing for the burial of a few failures.

Small changes in level can be difficult to identify, and what appears to be almost level ground can in fact have surprising level changes. This may not matter for areas of turf or garden beds, but if you plan to pave, these falls can be disconcerting. Paving needs to provide a sense of security and stability, while excessive slopes do not create this feeling. They are best addressed by means of a step at the interface of paving and other surfaces.

Small changes of this type are a nuisance, an inconvenience perhaps, but they are not a major challenge. As slopes become greater, however, the solution to them does become a challenge, and there are only certain responses available to us.

Sloping sites in small gardens are not usable, and given that we now see our garden as a useful extension of our home we need to try to modify slopes to our advantage. Terraces are the most realistic solution, for the great problem with a sloping block is that it cannot be used for most of the outdoor activities we enjoy. By creating terraces the garden designer does achieve usable space.

There are points to remember about the creation of terraces, though. Firstly, they need to be linked, and this calls for the use of steps. Make these sufficiently wide for comfortable passage, and ensure that they have effective traction. Wet slate steps, for example, can be dangerously slippery. Steps must also have a consistent dimension through any flight; in other words, the height of the riser and the width of the tread should remain the same, while for comfort they should fit a recognized formula of twice the riser plus the height of the tread being about 26–27in (650–675mm).

In the creation of terraces, do ensure that the cut made in the site is approximately equal to the fill required. You will be surprised at how time-consuming and expensive it is to move mass materials like excess clay. If you have restricted access to a town backyard this will also be very inconvenient, so retain material on-site if you can.

You will need to build retaining walls to establish your terraces, and these can be expensive. Large retaining walls need to be properly constructed to engineers' specifications, and all of this adds cost. Selecting materials can be a problem too. Cheaper materials may not look too good, but does it matter if they are to be covered by hanging plants anyway? Drainage is also essential when you build retaining walls, to reduce the load on the walls.

Planning a garden with terraces is the same as planning any other garden. You need to ensure that each terrace layer has sufficient space for your proposed activities. One terrace may, for example, be designed to accommodate tables and chairs for eating and entertaining. It might be an idea to design the terrace below to accommodate pattern gardens, so that you can look down on them.

Keep practical issues in mind when you organize terracing. If you store a lawnmower in a shed close to the house, avoid making the upper terrace into lawn, otherwise pulling the mower up and down will frustrate you at the least, and may cause greater strain as well.

The steeper the slopes involved, then, the more difficult your task. You may find that the top of a steep back garden gives you breathtaking views. What a place this would be to sit in and enjoy a meal! In such cases it may be worthwhile to build a small pavilion with electrical power connected for simple alfresco cooking so that you do not need to run up and down for tea or coffee — that sort of energetic journey would demand refreshment considerably stronger than tea!

There are, of course, situations that preclude the construction of terraces, for example where underlying geology prevents extensive earthworks, and in these cases the use of decking can be an absolute boon. Usually constructed of timber, decking can provide attractive level areas on a slope and in extreme circumstances it can protrude a long way out from a slope. There are sites where swimming pools have been built into steep slopes and surrounded by a deck built out from a hillside.

Always remember that there are safety issues to be faced wherever you have retaining walls or decks. A significant change in height demands that you offer some barrier. The easiest solution may be a hedge planting, though constructed barriers, especially if they are combined with climbing plants to soften them, can be effective. Clematis are excellent for this, but do avoid roses, as people naturally dislike leaning on them!

Where a series of small decking terraces are used on a hillside, there is enormous potential for enclosing these with dense planting so that each becomes an oasis among the vegetation. Remember that not all terraces need to be the same size. A large one may be used for entertaining, while a small one may be part of the stairs where a few tubs are placed for interest. In the design illustrated, a much less dramatic solution has been provided for a back yard with a slope from the back fence to the house, a change in level of close to 3ft (about 1m).

LEFT: Terraces have made this sloping site into a useful and attractive area. Softening planting is essential to reduce the impact of the hard surfaces.

The terraced garden

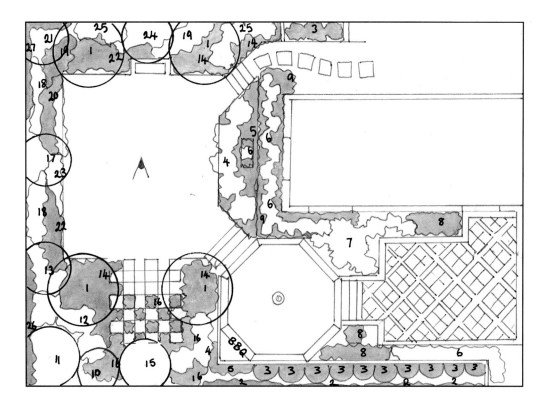

On this site three levels of garden are proposed, the first an extended paved area at the level of the house using a simple patterned paving. Steps carry the paving up 1ft (30cm) to an octagonal dining terrace that accommodates a barbecue. Remember that the construction of a series of retaining walls will be quite complex and expensive.

The upper level of the garden is largely lawn, and as such is designed to provide a sufficiently large area for children to play in. Here, also, is the opportunity for some patterned garden using pavers, gravel and plants.

The selection of plants for this garden include those able to tumble over the retaining walls to soften them and disguise their presence; they are, after all, quite intrusive. We have used *Convolvulus mauretanicus* and *Cotoneaster dammeri* to fulfil this role in this design. There is, however, an enormous range of plants that could be used: a low-grafted *Pyrus salicifolia* 'Pendula'; the prolific cover of *Hydrangea petiolaris* tumbling over walls from above; even climbers work well.

Note, in this design, how the height of the wall immediately behind the house is reduced by dividing it into two in such a way that plants from below can screen the wall behind. Use this approach, as unbroken walls can be very dominant.

The year-round garden

Attention has been drawn to the importance of selecting effective plants for your garden. The best of these contribute for an extended period of time so that, even in the bleakest of winter days, there are still highlights to enjoy in the garden. There is little bleaker than walking through a winter garden where there is hardly anything to be enjoyed. This problem becomes worse as winters become colder and the hours of daylight shorter. To overcome this problem, care is needed in the selection of plants.

In cold environments, where winter flower hues are scarce, the jasmine *Jasminum nudiflorum* is treated with great reverence. It does, after all, produce yellow, scented flowers through the winter. Where conditions are warmer, however, it is relatively infrequently planted, being so much less successful than the splendid *J. mesnyi*. Plant evaluation does vary depending upon your location. Where winters are less to be feared, gardens retain considerable display and variation of hues. This should be recognized when selecting plants. In warmer gardens

OPPOSITE: Where a garden is required to provide year-round interest paving takes on a key role. Timber, natural stone and cobbles will all offer decorative quality throughout the year.

there is little problem about achieving year-round brightness. Here plants like *Lavandula dentata* and *Euryops pectinatus* will flower throughout the year and indeed cause problems when it comes to deciding when to prune.

No such problem exists in cold climes for, of course, there is no similar willingness to flower the year through. Here careful selection of plants is vital. There is a need to consider not only the potential for winter flowers, but also the opportunity for differing shades from bark, foliage, fruit, and even the layers of branching in strongly layered plants.

Bark is a fine source of interest in the garden. No one who has enjoyed the bark of the birch can doubt this. Ghostly at night, it shimmers in the winter sun, especially in some of the choice species, such as *Betula utilis* var. *jacquemontii*. The combination of bark with plants ensures that seasonal microcosms are established. A carpet of *Cyclamen coum,* for example, beneath a birch, would have a special quality, as would a massing of another type of bulb such as *Crocus tomasinianus,* surely one of the greatest winter delights.

Many trees produce their best bark upon young wood, so it may be a worthwhile idea to encourage production of this young bark. The technique allowing this effect to be achieved is called coppicing. It is the

approach used to ensure that plants like the tinted, stemmed dogwoods and willows provide beauty for the winter garden. The plants that benefit from this treatment include *Cornus alba,* with red-brown stems, *C.a.* 'Elegantissima', with scarlet stems, 'Westonbirt', with bright red stems, and *C. stolonifera* 'Flaviramea', with yellowish green stems. Willows used for this effect include *Salix alba* 'Britzensis'.

Fruit can be highly decorative too, though most fruits do not last through the winter. The berries of cotoneasters and pyracanthas are well-known, but the dramatic lilac berries of *Callicarpa bodinieri giraldii* are less frequently seen. Selecting plants for fruit does not reduce the quality of your garden in any respect, for fruiting trees can also produce effective flowers: the selection of plants for fruit simply extends their decorative role. *Malus* 'Golden Hornet' and *M. hupehensis* are fine examples.

The use of evergreen plants is a vital aspect of the all-year garden. Do not restrict yourself to the use of green foliage plants, for there are many plants with variegated foliage worthy of cultivation. These may be out of fashion at the present time, however, they can be effective parts of any planting scheme, offering a warmth in winter and a contrast to the other greens of the garden. *Eleagnus pungens* 'Maculata', for example, is a first-class plant, dressed with a wonderful

gold foliage. *Euonymus fortunei* 'Variegatus' is another fine foliage plant, light and decorative and excellent for dressing the lower trunks of trees. Conifers, too, are good year-round trees. The golden cypress *Chamaecyparis pisifera* 'Filifera Aurea', the blue of Koster's blue spruce, *Picea pungens* 'Koster' and *Juniperus conferta* typify the quality of plants available for winter foliage.

Plants are not the sole source of interest for the winter, for garden furniture can also contribute effectively throughout the year. You can paint furniture so that it contributes to an overall scheme, or use glazed and patterned tiles, possibly as an edging of pools, at the base of pools or as a decorative element on walls. Such a scheme provides a more Mediterranean feel, and may be best related to the use of tubs of citrus, such as cumquat.

In smaller gardens the lack of space means that all planting must contribute to the year-round aspect. It not only allows the creation of the wonderful summer display so popular with gardeners, but also allows other areas to create a more even display. Note that there are many plants that look excellent in decline — grasses, for example, are splendid at the end of the season when their dry heads and stems add a most dramatic effect to a garden. Some plants do not justify being cut back until very late in the year, after they have provided a winter display.

LEFT: Lattice work and sculpture can both contribute to year-round quality of a garden so that even when deciduous foliage has fallen these non-plant features retain interest in the garden.

ABOVE: *A balance of evergreen and deciduous material is essential to achieve year-round interest. Bulbs can be used to augment flowering in spring and autumn while gravel will contribute colour and texture at all times.*

The year-round garden

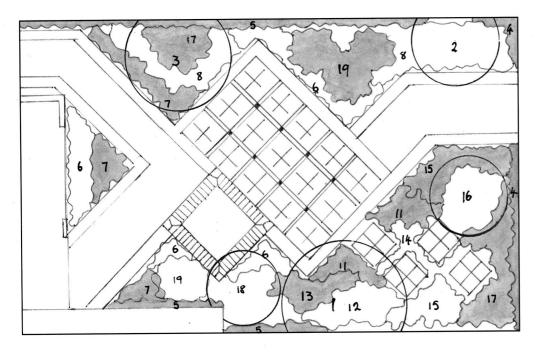

In this garden design, year-round interest has been provided by the quite strongly patterned paving, while the walls of the garden are covered by evergreen climbers. The tree selected to dominate the garden is *Photinia beauvardiana*, a small tree with considerable merit: its flowers, its summer and fall (autumn) foliage and handsome berries. Throughout the garden consideration has been given to using plants with good display at different times of the year. There is extensive opportunity for interplanting, the establishment, for example, of bulbs beneath ground-covers, and this results in each area of the garden providing at least two seasons of display.

In the design, note the use of a diagonal layout. This relates to the diagonal link between the house and the door in the rear wall, but also results in effective planting spaces. Locating functional elements in a garden of this size is never easy, but a clothesline has been established in the shelter of the tree. Paving for sitting borders the pool so a raised pool edge has been created to prevent chairs from slipping into the pool. In small spaces of this type, a simple design is frequently the best solution.

The balcony garden

More and more people are living in high-rise buildings in cities. Many of their homes have balconies, while others have access to roof spaces. All of these spaces have features in common, most notably no natural ground water, no access to open soil, and exposure to significant wind currents, the sun, and views.

Having such spaces available is a most attractive feature of an apartment, for they can certainly provide contact with nature, and the opportunity to grow plants for display and visual enjoyment as well as for the kitchen. The cultivation of a few herbs and salad crops is a major attraction for any gardener living in such a situation, and is not a difficult task. If the gardener recognizes the prevailing conditions, plants can be grown very successfully on a balcony or rooftop.

The modification of microclimates is the first essential, for use by both yourself and your plants. Unfortunately, it is not possible to use large masses of vegetation to achieve this effect. After all, there is nowhere for it to root, and as it becomes larger above the ground but its root system remains small, its stability in the wind will be threatened. Note that larger plants have more foliage and, therefore, a greater need for water. In roof gardens of any type it is difficult to see where this water will come from, especially as plants are grown in containers. Water will need to be added to the root zone of the

ABOVE: *Even a tiny balcony becomes an attractive retreat with some rose-covered lattice.*

OPPOSITE: *A small balcony or roof garden can provide an exciting outdoor room where every bit of space is vital to the overall effect. For lush growth, adequate water provision is absolutely essential.*

plant at a rate sufficient to compensate for water loss, something that is difficult to achieve with larger specimens.

Plants on the rooftop or balcony are unlikely to provide most of our climate protection. You will need to use constructed elements, such as blinds drawn out over sitting areas to create shade, or light lattices to establish both privacy and wind protection. Note that wind protection also implies wind resistance, and too large a screen may well be blown over in extreme conditions.

Containers are essential for all plants cultivated on balconies, but they need to have good irrigation and effective drainage. They need not be especially deep. Given a small balcony or roof space, my first priority would be a salad or herb garden, where I could grow parsley, lettuce, chives, basil, and the other plants so easy to cultivate and so useful in the kitchen. These need no more than, say, a container 4–6in (10–15cm) deep, and this could be created from a few planks, used as a rectangular bed. Fill the bed with an open potting mix (available with water-retaining granules and nutrients already mixed in), and then irrigate with a plastic drip irrigation system. Gravel, so regularly recommended for the bases of pots, is not needed here, for it tends to impede drainage, but effective irrigation will be necessary to ensure that the water supply to the plants is kept up. It is a good idea to use a water sensor in these conditions. This senses the water content of the potting mix, and switches the irrigation system on automatically when it falls to a critical level.

Your rooftop salad garden could be augmented by other crops in pots. Try tomatoes, that never taste so good from shops as they do when grown at home, and perhaps some beans, grown as a decorative climber on a lattice against a wall, or rosemary and sage, grown in containers as decorative plants. Even try growing some delicious fruit — cumquats, lemons and new dwarf apples, for example 'Ballerina' — to make a large balcony garden more productive. It may not be possible to have an entirely self-sufficient fruit and vegetable garden on a balcony, but the cultivation of a few productive plants will give you great satisfaction. Herb plants are generally enormously attractive, and because of their Mediterranean origins they can be grown in soils that are quite dry. Even one of our largest herbs, the bay, could be grown as a clipped specimen in a container.

Many of the options you could pursue on your balcony garden depend upon its size. Given a small balcony without sufficient space to sit, I would grow mostly tubs of ornamental plants, with a few herbs. For a larger balcony, my preference would be for more herbs, with only a few decorative containers. A larger balcony still would mean room for both herbs and decorative plants.

The balcony garden

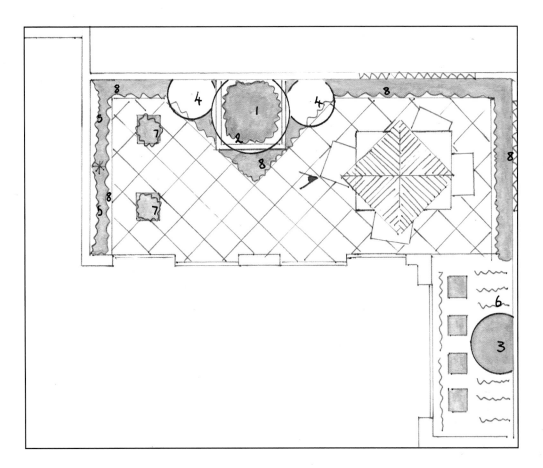

Key to planting

1. *Fortunella margarita*
2. *Ophiopogon japonicus*
3. *Laurus nobilis*
4. *Rosmarinus officinalis*
5. *Mandevilla laxa*
6. Herb and vegetable garden including:
   Capsicum annuum 'California Wonder'
   (Capsicum)
   Ocimum basilicum 'Spicy Globe' (Basil)
   Petroselinum crispum 'Triple Curled'
   (Parsley)
   Latuca sativa 'Green Oakleaf' and
   'Red Oakleaf' (Lettuce)
7. Containers planted for seasonal colour:
   e.g. *Foeniculum vulgare* 'Purpureum'
   Chrysanthemum mawii
8. Seasonal planting display to be altered
   seasonally:
   Petunia 'Dreams White'

In this plan, the space allows for a dining table to be set up outside, and a few vegetables and tubs of decorative plants.

With the open site characteristic of a rooftop setting, it is essential to use plants sufficiently tough to tolerate exposure to the sun, wind and cold. However, cold may not be quite such a problem in city areas as it is in the country, because of the heat emanating from the city itself; this keeps temperatures a few degrees higher.

Base your planting around a few permanent display plants in tubs or hanging baskets, and then change your display planting with the seasons, and from year to year. The plantings suggested in this plan would be fine for a single season in the first year, but next year you would want something fresh. This might be seen as an expensive approach to gardening, but the fact is that you will not need many plants — you have only a restricted area in which to garden.

Note that while there is no real possibility of using a large water feature, not least because of its weight, I have included a beautifully patterned tub filled with water as part of the display. A large and dramatic bunch of flowers, or just a few floating blossoms, could be put here for parties. Sculpture, too, is an exciting element in such gardens.

The narrow garden

Gaining privacy in small gardens is never easy, especially in narrow gardens in densely populated areas where adjacent buildings appear to intrude not only into the space but also into rooms within our homes. Much of this intrusion is purely imaginary, but the very thought of being overlooked is unpleasant. At the same time, narrow long spaces appear as corridors, especially with an adjacent block containing taller buildings. Long, bleak corridor spaces are daunting at all times, yet they can be made more acceptable.

Firstly, consider the long space as a series of spaces, able to be broken up in one way or another. On one occasion, where the problem was a narrow side garden and space permitted, I created a series of courtyards outside bedrooms, where teenage children and parents had their own outdoor rooms,

OPPOSITE: Narrow gardens are always difficult. This delightful treatment so fills the garden that its narrowness is no longer apparent, rather the fulsome colour of geraniums, roses and catmint and the charming colour of the neighbouring houses' facades attract attention.

decorated with schemes of flower and foliage to suit their needs. The children enjoyed a jungle of large-leaved plants, the parents a garden of subtle tones of grey, green and white. Combining the development of the architecture with that of the garden scheme was especially worthwhile.

Too frequently, architectural works are considered independent of garden design. Yet there is much to be said for employing garden designers together with architects, or at least ensuring that your architect works sympathetically in relation to your garden, for buildings and gardens feed off each other.

A less formal solution than the set of courtyards might suit you. Do not run a path through as a single line of pavers; rather break it into a series of short paths that cut back and forth across the width of the garden. Each short length of path can focus upon a feature plant, or even a small sculpture. Spaces between the path and the house or the fence can be filled with planting. Remember, too, that trees used to create a screen will take a lot of space. They will also not be able to provide a screen immediately unless you buy very tall specimens, and these are expensive. Leaf fall may also lead to clogged gutters, and then

you have the bothersome task of emptying them. Large trees are likely to make these side gardens darker and more drear.

Lattice will do fine. Try to avoid making it appear an add-on to an existing fence. Rather run it from ground level over the face of the fence to the height you need. In extremes, use a wire tennis court fence covered with a quick-growing evergreen climber such as *Pandorea pandorana* or *Muehlenbeckia complexa*. Tennis court fences will need to be continuous, but lattice panels need not be, and they can be used only in areas where they are protecting windows.

Try putting a ceiling over your narrow space to prevent visibility from higher windows. There is no need to cover the whole area, but a light pergola structure above windows will help to provide privacy for them without taking all the light. Whenever possible, place your pergola timbers at the angle of the house roof. Our eyes will tend to link each of the pergolas to the other, so that though the area may not be completely covered, our mental combination of all the individual canopies will give a great sense of shelter. For homes with two floors, have climbers on the pergola, so that upper windows can overlook flower displays.

The narrow garden

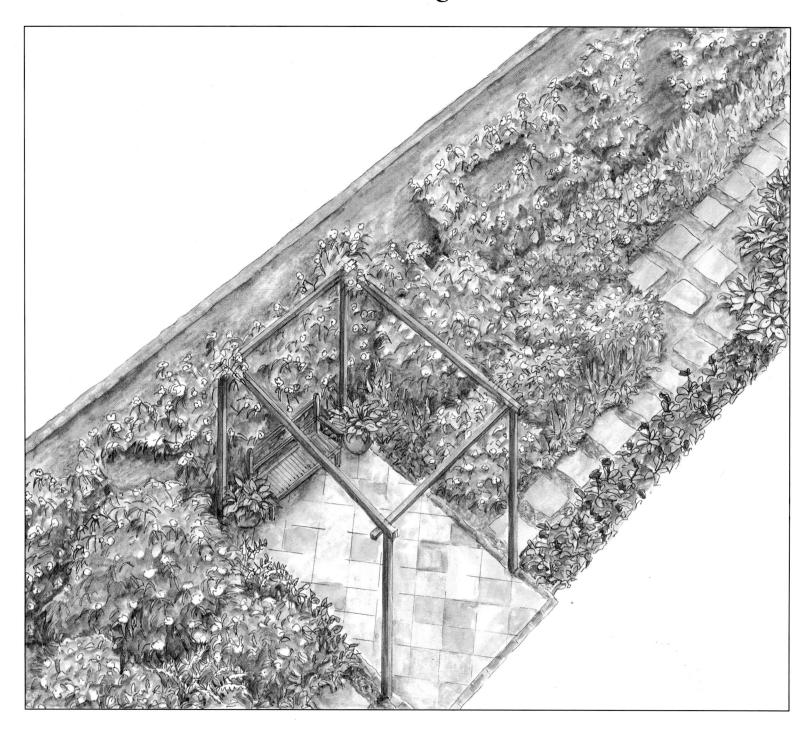

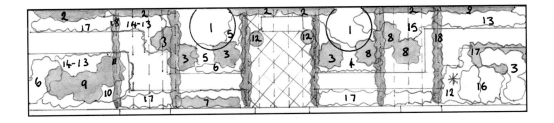

Key to planting

1. *Viburnum rhytidiphyllum*
2. *Camellia sasanqua* (espaliered)
3. *Skimmia japonica* (male and female plants)
4. *Tellima grandiflora*
5. *Polygonatum* x *hybridum*
6. *Epimedium warleyense*
7. *Cotoneaster horizontalis*
8. *Hydrangea quercifolia*
9. *Mahonia* x *media* 'Charity'
10. *Omphalodes verna*
11. *Omphalodes verna*
12. *Hosta sieboldiana* 'Elgans' underplanted with *Eranthis hyemalis*
13. *Euphorbia robbiae*
14. Interplanted in 13 *Dianella tasmanica*
15. *Anemone japonica* 'Queen Charlotte'
16. *Garrya elliptica* 'James Roof'
17. *Bergenia* 'Sunningdale'
18. *Trachelospermum jasminoides*

This relatively narrow side passageway is overlooked by an adjacent house to the east. The objective of the design is to reduce the feeling of a throughway and lessen the impact of the adjacent house by providing separate canopies to windows; these create an effective ceiling to the space. Wooden pergolas have been used, except over a central sitting space, where timbers bear strained wires with delicate climbers, which give a lighter cover.

Large pavers form a path, assuring adequate space for passage; ground-covers grow over their edge. The path is staggered by having the pavers laid as diagonals at crossing points; thus a series of spaces is created. Most important, at the midpoint of the path there is a paved area for a seat and tubs, as much a focus to the view from the windows as a place to sit quietly and read. This area provides an important space in the throughway.

The critical element of this garden is its luxuriance and softness. Sufficient internal interest is also established to draw the eye from the unsightly buildings. Texture and year-round flowers are vital here. The evergreen shrubs *Mahonia* x *media* 'Charity', *Viburnum rhytidiphyllum* and *Garrya elliptica* 'James Roof' fill these requirements, while many of the ground-covers, including *Epimedium warleyense,* *Euphorbia robbiae* and *Bergenia* 'Sunningdale', add to the effect. The fence is screened by the use of espaliered camellias, an ideal narrow belt of evergreen foliage, its effect assisted by tying the plants against strained wires on the fence.

Flowers are augmented by excellent fruit, notably on the *Skimmia japonica,* for which male and female plants have been planted. Changing hues of the foliage of epimediums, *Bergenia* 'Sunningdale' and *Hydrangea quercifolia*, are augmented in fall (autumn) by the display of the Japanese windflower 'Queen Charlotte', a delightful pink flower that spreads quickly to fill the rear of planting areas.

CREATING PRIVACY & SECLUSION

Your garden haven

A small garden is your retreat, a special haven available to you and your family. It is only natural for you to want to make it private from prying eyes. In cities, attention can come from all directions, and not just people living next door, for with high-rise buildings views may come from some distance. Equally, you may wish for some internal privacy, dividing your garden to provide you with a place to sit and read or sunbathe away from the general view of the rest of your family.

STRUCTURES FOR SCREENING

The use of plants and structures to achieve privacy is an imperative, and because of a lack of space most of these, whether vertical or horizontal, need to be carefully considered so that they do not occupy too much space. Occasionally a tree such as a jacaranda or Chinese elm may be suitable, its branches forming an overhead umbrella, but do remember that even if it is planted as a

OPPOSITE: A protected sitting area becomes especially important where a garden is overlooked. Even a small sitting area of this type can be a haven in the city.

PREVIOUS PAGE: Where privacy is established with dense planting, an outdoor terrace or a conservatory can provide a delightful garden feature. Pots suitably filled add to the charm of this garden.

mature specimen a tree will take time to give effective cover. (You may also have trouble getting a mature specimen into a rear garden without access.)

In contrast, structural screening can be immediate — pergolas and lattice, for example, offer instantaneous screening, even if the climbers that will cover them take a year or two to grow over. While you may be patient with some parts of the garden, screening is likely to be one of your first priorities. Walls, fences, lattice and pergolas are all useful for this, though they may be more expensive than plants. Privacy is achieved either by overhead or vertical screens, and it is vital that you decide which you need. Consider the maintenance needs of a screen from the beginning: plants on it may need to be pruned and trained, and timber, once painted, may need to be repainted, not always an easy or welcome task.

Vertical screens provide a block to views from the side. They are ideal when you want privacy from rooms adjacent to your garden, or privacy within your garden. You may find that they need to be constructed as a result of a joint effort by you and the home-owner next door. Both of you will often have the same desire for screening, in which case you are fortunate because no conflicts will arise. Problems do come when you try to screen people living next door who do not wish to see a screen — after all, it may shade

their garden. Solid screens are not the best solution in such cases, and you may do best to resort to vegetation.

Critical to your need to create privacy is the need to retain light and sun entry. You will have to decide between the two, as design is after all a series of compromises to achieve the best solution in the circumstances. If you do choose to use plants, remember the implications of the roots of large trees. They can do a lot of damage, for which you will be legally responsible. Frequently, the use of a light structure with a less vigorous but trained plant will give the best result.

The decision whether to use brick or some other masonry material, timber or lattice will depend upon individual choice. Materials used in the past in your garden are likely to have been of local origin, so for older homes these may still be the best option. However, the ease of transport today means we can look further afield. Start with a trip to a local garden supply store to see the range of materials available. Try to relate the look, scale and texture of the material you are choosing to your building materials, if need be, treating your side walls with paint or mortar to achieve a consistency of finish. Climbing plants can help too, especially evergreens like Chinese star jasmine, though self-clingers like climbing fig are always easier to look after.

Masonry is likely to be more expensive than timber or lattice, but it does last, and its maintenance is less demanding. It also reduces noise, and in areas with houses close together this can be a boon. A small fountain can also be used. This will not reduce noise, but may mask it — this is always a good alternative. Remember, if you are building masonry, to build in any services you need — power and water for fountains, power for light, piping for irrigation, and so on. Try to foresee future needs. You may also design your wall to display an effective brick pattern or a treasured wall sculpture, or glazed tiles. Have freestanding walls professionally designed; a collapsing wall is dangerous. Do be aware that walls can cause wind turbulence, so consider their exposure to winds and the detrimental effect this could have on your enjoyment of your garden.

Timbers have a relatively high maintenance requirement, and a shorter life than masonry, but they can be covered with climbers and offer an excellent frame. Money spent at the outset buying more durable timber is money well spent, since cheaper softwoods rot more quickly. Ensure that cut ends of wood are all treated to prevent the entry of rots. Use wood preservatives and paints. I enjoy the weathered shades of natural timbers, but painting can contribute to an effective and stylish overall scheme. Remember, though, that if you paint timber, repainting can be extremely difficult once the screen is covered by climbers.

Where there is too much wall or a need to screen, lattice can be really useful. Buy good-quality lattice, and give it an effective frame to strengthen it visually and secure it against the damage caused by rampant climbers and wind and weather. Lattice can have a square or a diamond pattern. I prefer the former, as it is more classical in its feel, but a diamond pattern may reflect diagonal lines used in paving.

Never overlook the potential of strained wires for climbers. They may be used as an extension above a fence to gain height without excessive shadow. A light tracery of climbers on wire is excellent, but you will need to use a turn-buckle mechanism that will allow tightening of the wire from time to time. I like to use wire against climbing posts for voracious climbers like wisteria — otherwise their energetic growth can lead to the destruction of your timber posts.

Wire can also contribute to the provision of an overhead canopy, but only if climbers like Chinese star jasmine are grown over them. Privacy could be achieved above with a solid screen: by roofing in part of the garden. Use of a gazebo might be a solution here, but I prefer a light overhead canopy, offering a degree of privacy and some light

ABOVE: The entrance to any garden is important. Clipped hedges offer sentinels beside a charming cottage gate. Brick paving leads directly to the door, without pattern or fuss, but is effective, creating a simple sense of direction and distance.

entry. Be aware of the value of shadows in a garden, and enjoy the summer filigree pattern of shade as it moves across paving. Where winters are long and bleak, a deciduous climber, such as a clematis, would be excellent, for you do want as much winter light entry as possible, but where privacy is more important then a combination of an evergreen and a deciduous climber might be better.

Greatest overhead control will come from the use of a structured canopy. The use of timber squares dropped into a pre-fabricated structure would be excellent, providing you have somewhere to store them — in a shed, in the cellar, or in a hinged seat that permits storage underneath. The degree of light entry is directly proportional to the amount of canopy, so you can control light and privacy throughout the year.

HEDGES FOR PRIVACY

Hedges and climbers are ideal for screening because they grow upward and occupy relatively little space. Avoid hedges with prodigious growth, for example, cypress trees. In a few years they will cover a considerable width of your garden; rather use plants you can clip tight against a fence. It is for this reason that I like clipped climbers on wires next to a fence because they can be kept tighter. Plants like potato creeper and bower of beauty are excellent for this. Whichever solution you use, choose plants with small leaves. There are two reasons for this — firstly, they look better when clipped as you avoid the appearance of chewed half-leaves, and secondly, they provide a really effective background for your more strongly textured feature planting.

Hedges are, after all, only backgrounds to your scheme, filling a functional role. They are not a feature in their own right.

Remember that hedges have extensive roots. As you prune them you are frequently stimulating new growth and removing nutrients that would otherwise fall to the ground for recycling to compensate for this. The shaded and dry areas beneath them are difficult to plant. *Iris foetidissima,* dwarf cyclamen and hellebores are very effective

in these circumstances. Feed hedges to ensure that they retain sufficient vigour, and recognize that their roots will draw water from the surrounding ground, making life more difficult for more interesting, cherished plants. Irrigation can help compensate here.

Avoid bulky coniferous hedges. They occupy too much space. While they grow fast, they soon create shade and a very firm line, reinforcing the smallness of your plot.

ABOVE: *Lush climbers covering fences create a similar effect to hedges except that they are looser and therefore less formal. This visually rich scheme offers a perfect retreat from the adjacent urban landscape and gives privacy for its occupants. The stone orbs on the fence top strongly delineate the garden boundary.*

SURFACES
FOR THE SMALL
GARDEN

The value of paving

Plants are generally thought of as the most decorative elements of a garden, yet many may have a beauty that is transient: a flush of flowers or a fire of foliage before returning to a less exotic and less appealing state. Paving, by contrast, is a consistent feature, though even this may look different at times; for example, it may look better wet than dry. But the pattern and tones you choose to use will remain the same, offering an excellent foil for plant foliages, and an opportunity to create line to carry your eyes about the garden, so that you explore dominant areas and look to focal points. Furthermore, the texture of paving is exciting, especially if contrasted with that of foliage. Here lies the opportunity to be a sculptor with plants and paving, an exciting challenge that is taken up by the finest garden designers.

OPPOSITE: The use of patterned paving permits the integration of planting and paving. Gravels also allow a softness well suited to a combination of plants and hard surfaces as is being used in this garden.

PREVIOUS PAGE: Use of paving can avoid the use of grass in a small garden though that does not imply that the garden need be hard and unattractive. Massed planting and effective textures ensure that the garden retains a softness and charm.

Yet, too frequently, paving is laid without any thought to its real contribution to the garden. Good paving starts at the planning stage, and should be thought through carefully to ensure that pattern and line can be developed in the space available.

Start your paving by considering the way it can help with the design of your garden. For example, it may be used to reflect the angled shape of part of your house. Remember also that diagonal lines will be longer than those at 90° to the garden axis. You may be able to use these lines across a garden to lead the eye and to achieve an effect of greater size, both important in the small garden.

Be careful to avoid a small paving scale. If your garden is small, this does not always mean that you should choose small-unit pavers. Equally, make sure that paved areas are large enough to fulfil their functions. Paths, for example, need to accommodate both you and a wheelbarrow, or you and a friend. A minimum width of 4ft (1.2m) is desirable. If you see that the edge of the path is being softened by tumbling plants from either side, then it may need to be 6ft (1.8m) wide.

Make outdoor eating areas large enough to accommodate a space comfortable for relaxing, and perhaps a barbecue. It is a good idea to mark out such an area with lime before deciding on its final size, and pretend to use it, so that you can see if it

really works. Remember that this kind of area needs to be entirely open and usable. A pond or fountain in the middle may be an attractive option, but will destroy the usefulness of the space. Place other features such as these at the edge. Sitting outside is more relaxing and therefore demands more space than sitting inside.

Your path may appear to be the size of an airport runway through your site when it is new, but it will suit the scale of the garden as soon as plants start growing over it. A few strong pieces of paving will look better than obviously narrow paths. Use pavers of a scale suited to their setting. You may use a small paver, for example a brick, to create a pattern, and then in-fill with a larger paver. In such cases it is the scale of the grid that will read, not that of the brick.

Take care to ensure that clear and effective paving is laid to your front door. This is where your visitors will arrive at your house, and the paving needs to be welcoming. Any steps here should be lit — remember that first-time visitors will not know the vagaries of your site. I like to have a wider paved plinth immediately in front of the door, where friends can stand to be welcomed and farewelled.

Small gardens appear larger if ground textures are smooth. Avoid long grass, for example — it appears to fill the garden, making it look smaller. A well-cut lawn will appear more spacious. Avoid, too, the use of serpentine lawns. It is far better to have strong geometrics, circles and arcs, or effectively used straight lines that are sharp and give a sense of space. In-fill around these with decorative planting, to create spaces and softness. This will help enlarge your garden.

Selecting your paving material depends upon several factors. Local availability is important, and so is suitability for your context; for example, ask whether the paving materials suit the building materials of the house. You may extend an internal paver outside, but be careful. Terracotta will be fine in warm climates, but not where there are frosts, when it quickly breaks up. In general, building materials are subjected to far worse conditions when on the ground than when used in buildings. Not only is there the wear of feet to consider, but the materials also stay wet longer, and may be subject to freezing and thawing and the impact of the sun.

Look around at nearby gardens to see what works well, and visit suppliers and especially scrap yards and second-hand dealers, because they can often offer out-of-the-ordinary or recycled materials that might otherwise be too expensive. Consider the use of flamboyant materials for zest and life. Glazed tiles make excellent highlights in a paving scheme, and can be continued into the base of an ornamental pond, a mosaic or even the surface of a table. Careful searching may help you locate pots with a tint similar to the glaze that will establish an effective design link.

Natural stones are among the loveliest of paving materials, but they are expensive. In small areas you may need so little that economics are not a significant feature anyway. But remember that you may need to consider the cost of laying the paving as well, and this can double the cost of the material. It is important to see the cost involved in establishing a garden in the context of your house's resale value. Those in the know suggest that expenditure of 8 to 10 percent of house value on the development of the garden will be recouped. Keep this in mind when you consider your budget for garden building.

GRAVELS

I generally avoid the use of random paving in small gardens. The busyness of the pattern that results is often disappointing. Sawn stones are a delight to use, however. Where most proprietary products have a consistency of size and texture, natural stones reveal all of the vagaries of nature, and this imbues them with a life absent from even the most expensive manufactured pavers. If natural stone paving costs too much, you might consider using cobbles or gravels for textural change. Gravels are the smallest natural pavers you are likely to obtain. Used beneath and around a container or sculpture, they can offer a delightful contrast. The now popular grasses are a wonderful contrast to the rounded shapes of river cobbles, the linear foliage erupting from within the cobbles.

Gravels offer a relatively inexpensive way of covering the ground. Plants can grow through them — try dwarf bulbs such as *Narcissus bulbocodium* or gladioli — so that hard edges between paving and planting become delightfully soft and tend to flow into each other. Gravels can also provide a filler for gaps between pavers, so that there is again a contrast. Be aware that where children play, gravel can get scuffed about. Loose gravel on paths is ideal for

them to play with: they can bulldoze it into piles and then level it again — but it does require discipline to ensure the gravel is not spread further afield.

GRASSES

Grass has become a ubiquitous element in the garden. It is its softness, its relatively easy maintenance and its good tones that have made it so popular. Yet many fine smaller gardens have no grass, and there is much to be said for its omission unless you really need it. Children enjoy it, and its surface is quite yielding for them, but it does not really tolerate heavy wear well, especially where it is shaded and poorly drained — here moss and bare patches can take over. Storage of a lawnmower is a further problem where space is restricted, so you might do best to avoid the need for it altogether.

Where you do decide to use grass, I would edge it so that it becomes a bold landscape element. Circled with brick, concrete pavers or some other pavers, herbaceous plants can tumble without causing difficulties in mowing and without killing areas of lawn. Furthermore, the lawn will be focussed and strengthened within the design.

The normal lawn consists of grass, but some may be tempted to use herbs, which offer scent and flower. Thyme, chamomile and mint have been used as lawns; all need sun and good drainage. But even in optimal conditions the weed seed bank in the ground tends to take over, and these lawns become a maintenance headache. If you really want to enjoy the herb turfs, then use them as raised seats within brick retaining walls. You can provide good drainage, design them to be in the sun, and clip and weed them easily because you need not bend. This will be a relief — the ground always seems far too low anyway.

GROUND-COVERS

Where shade is a problem, the delightful Baby's Breath *(Helxine soleirolii)* is likely to grow if conditions are moist. Mosses, too, are likely to grow, and I enjoy these. Both plant types are soft and pretty, and you are better off going with the flow rather than changing things to make grass grow here.

Areas of low-growing planting have important roles to play in small gardens. They can offer good texture, and allow views across them, so that a garden may be explored in full. Look for evergreen plants with attractive foliage so that their quality is visible throughout the year. Ivies *(Hedera* sp.) are the most ubiquitous of these covers, but they are not necessarily the best looking, although they are very shade tolerant. Look at the possibility of using mondo grass *(Ophiopogon japonicus)* or turf lily *(Liriope* sp.), with grassy leaves of excellent year-round texture and form. As with turf, the best effects are achieved from these plants when they are used en masse, though they can also offer the opportunity to use emergent textures as a contrast. It is much better to use a really tough plant in these situations than to struggle with something better looking but far more fragile.

Slopes offer a specific problem. My preference is to build retaining walls and to create terraces, but where this is too costly the use of ground-covering plants can be effective. This will reduce weed growth and hold the soil together to prevent erosion. Use plants with a good dense foliage and effective fibrous root system to do this. See Chapter Seven for more about planting on sloping sites.

Ground-cover plants provide the base plane of your garden. They have great value throughout the site, for holding together the divergent masses of plants you use. This visual consistency they achieve is vitally important in your design; it ensures that the ground is clothed and offers a contrast to your dominant foliages. In such circumstances, bear in mind my comments about hedges. These are background plants for the stars, the supporting cast, whose role is to be seen but not to shine! Similarly, many ground-cover plants will plug away happily in a secondary role. Elsewhere, where their texture is important, they will become stars in their own right. Plants such as *Bergenia* sp. and *Pachysandra terminalis* are excellent here.

ABOVE: Gravels and low planting give the opportunity to interesting textural combinations in a garden, a quality that has been built on here where textural masses form the focus to the garden.

PLANTING FOR FRAGRANCE & DELIGHT

Selecting plants for balance

Few of us fail to fall under the spell of plants. We probably have special childhood memories of our parents' or grandparents' gardens being filled with evocative smells, the buzz and movement of insects or the call of birds. Such is the power of plants and especially their flowers that we may find ourselves choosing plants for our gardens simply for emotional reasons — for their familiarity and their role in our early lives.

While there is no harm in such a basis for plant selection, we should also realize that a small garden calls for the use of plants of outstanding merit and an ability to perform consistently for our pleasure and enjoyment. Impulse buying at nurseries does not assure us of the best; we need to research, assess and evaluate, thinking of plants not

OPPOSITE: Repetition of plants to achieve symmetry gives balance and a focus to a viewline. The focus in this garden is achieved by use of a low urn of Lamium galeobdalon *'Herman's Pride' and the beautifully textured* Itea ilicifolia.

PREVIOUS PAGE: The effect of plant layers is beautifully shown in this combination of tulips and forget-me-nots. Similar effects can be achieved by careful selection of perennials and shrubs especially if flowering combinations of an emergent and a base planting can be established.

as individuals, but as opportunities — they can be combined and integrated into garden pictures. Where seasonal plants are used, consider others that will fill their place in their down season. The most exciting planting schemes work on this basis.

Study effective planting in other gardens. Note that many plants are used repeatedly in sizeable groups, and that only the largest plants tend to be used as single specimens or critical focus plants, offering a kind of sculptural effect as an alternative to a sculpture itself. Repeat planting is especially useful with background plantings like hedges or ground-covers, where the consistency created is an important part of the design.

Note also that in effectively planted gardens there is often a repetition of key plants through the design. This repetition helps to achieve a cohesion in the design and can contribute significantly to the visual satisfaction gained from any garden. I use evergreen plants to fill this role so that this continuity is retained throughout the year.

You can achieve balance with planting. Symmetry may be essential for the most formal gardens, where each side is a mirror image of the other, but such a need is rare in small gardens. It can work, though, for example if a courtyard or patio garden is given over entirely to a swimming pool or where a dominant pattern is needed for viewing from above.

Some other types of gardens will be asymmetrical; the halves will balance, but may not necessarily reflect each other completely. Look along the length of your garden from the house. A single tree to the left may need to be balanced by a group of shrubs to the right. Consider the volumes contained by the plants you are using, and ensure that they will balance each other on different sides of the garden. In these circumstances you will need to consider how many samples of a smaller plant to use for it to read effectively in the context of a larger specimen. Without grouping it will make no impact whatsoever in the design. Also use individual little treasures in containers where you can get near to them and enjoy their special qualities. Bring them inside if you wish to appreciate them more closely. Otherwise, group plants to achieve real effect from smaller plants.

Identifying the values of plants is not difficult. Look for good flower producers. Flowers are likely to be the basis of any sophisticated plant scheme you choose. White flowers might be especially attractive outside a bedroom or dining room where you will view them at night. Hot oranges and yellows with blue for an exciting contrast would be great for an outdoor summer eating area. If you intend to use this type of scheme, do make sure the plants you choose will flower together in your environment, otherwise your design effort will be wasted.

FOLIAGE FOR FLAMBOYANCE

Flowers should be augmented in these schemes by foliage. Never forget that green in its many shades will dominate in any garden. Indeed, a garden of greens, from yellow-greens through the spectrum to blue-greens and grey-greens, would seem to me to offer the most pleasing garden. Flowers would be almost superfluous, and could even be an intrusion!

Choosing some of the more flamboyant plants may create difficulties, as they may have poor foliage and form. Some of the roses are among this group, for while their flowers shriek romance and charm, their structure lacks the quality we should seek. Part of the solution is to mask them with better foliage plants, by what we might call "crush" planting, but we should also ensure we get recurrent flowering types so that our display is as effective as possible. Look, too, for those producing attractive hips to carry their display into the winter, such as *Rosa moyesii* and its cultivars, or the delightful *R. rugosa*. Such fruit can bring an extra dimension into our gardens by attracting birds in search of a winter feed.

Foliage can also be purple, silver, yellow or red, and the use of these tones can contribute effectively to planting schemes. The purple leaf of the smoke bush (*Cotinus coggygria* 'Notcutts Variety') is a superb element in a red planting. It could also look wonderful with the pinks of roses and with silver foliage. Much of your foliage display will last longer than any flowering, so you can enjoy its pleasures through an extended season, though fall (autumn) and spring foliage displays are briefer. The seasonal changes that these foliage displays represent are vital parts of the contact with

*ABOVE: The grey, delicate foliage of the weeping pear (*Pyrus salicifolia* 'Pendula') and variegated leaf of a hosta provide rich textural elements in combination with clipped box. The square of clipped box gives a most attractive formality to the whole combination.*

nature that gardens offer in towns and cities. Enjoy them to the full.

Foliage offers more than striking hues. Also recognize the value of foliage texture, and differentiate between the various types of leaf textures. The outer edge of the plant foliage might be described as its architectural texture. It is the strength of this that attracts our attention and gives the plant much of its quality. Plants with a strong architectural texture are useful against a

bland background, for example a painted wall or a hedge with fine foliage. Look at the splendid mahonia (*Mahonia lomariifolia*) to see this type of plant at its best, and consider how glorious it is when carefully underlit to cast shadow against a wall. Given that this plant also offers outstanding flower and fruit, its garden worthiness is quickly apparent. It is this ability to perform on many levels that makes a garden plant worthy of inclusion in our small garden.

ABOVE: Textures of foliage can provide enormous interest in a garden. Melianthus major, *with its grey-green divided leaves dominates (its foliage is unpleasantly scented) and its reddish purple flower bracts would relate well to the red-purple sheen of the New Zealand flax in the foreground.*

light shines on it. Plants used in deep shade will lose much of this quality. Many plants with strong surface textures also have architectural leaf shapes, so here you get the best of both worlds. Look at rodgersias, hostas and heucheras to appreciate the effect that such plants can have, but avoid using them on their own — their foliages need to be contrasted with those less obviously bold. Among climbing plants with this quality, I enjoy the Japanese climbing grape *(Vitis coignetiae),* not just for its foliage form and texture but also for its rich winey red fall (autumn) tint.

Do be careful when using the gaudy dwarf conifers with their foliage of dynamic steely blue or golden yellow-greens. Used in great diversity, they can provide patchy effects not to be encouraged in the smaller town garden.

PERFUMES FOR PERFECTION

The perfumes or scents of plants linger in our minds just as they can linger on our clothing. Who does not remember evocative childhood smells, suddenly recognized again when a brief waft is caught in the wind? There is something special about a garden of scents, whether the scents come from flowers, foliage or even fruit. Mow over a lemon when you next cut your grass, and the day will be made more pleasant by its lingering smell. Use scented plants effectively. For example, I like to have rosemary *(Rosmarinus officinalis)* where I sit so I can rub its foliage with my hands. If this is growing close to where I cook outside so much the better, because it is vital for barbecuing.

Rosemary is a plant with a good appearance, but other scented plants may

Foliage from climbing plants is especially critical since it allows a close contrast between the rigidity of the built structure and the flowing quality of the natural structure. Some of the ivies *(Hedera)* are ideal here, but I especially like the creeper *Parthenocissus henryana*, with its silver and pink variegation on the mid-rib and leaf veins.

Leaf variegation is not fashionable at present, though there are many plants

able to contribute much to the garden through their foliage variation. Look at the variegated hostas, ivies, and grasses to see how effective they can be, but do avoid those that appear to be in two minds about their health!

The leaf surface also has texture — either the leaf itself will be textured, or leaf hairs will create the texture. Leaf texture can be widely usable in your garden, but its usefulness does depend upon how much be less attractive. Allspice (*Chimonanthus praecox*), for example, has little beauty beyond its heady spring scent. Tuck it away in a corner where its weaknesses may be hidden, but where you can open french doors and be intoxicated by its perfume on a warm spring morning.

The heady perfumes of plant foliage can be superb, reminding us of vacations by the Mediterranean, where so many of these foliage plants originate. The heavy scents are a feature of not only the European Mediterranean plants, but also of plants from other areas with mediterranean climates, such as the eucalypts of Australia or Californian plants. Note how it is the young foliage of plants such as these that are especially lovely, so do not be too concerned if frost cuts the foliage down to the ground. On regrowth, the new young foliage will more than compensate for this loss. Many foliage plants look better for being rejuvenated, for younger foliage is often brighter and more attractive.

THE BEAUTY OF BARK

Gardeners rarely think sufficiently about the qualities of trunks as sources of interest. Birches are popular and useful garden trees for the beauty of their trunks, but there are also many others able to supply a splendid year-round effect. The Tibetan cherry (*Prunus serrula*) provides a bark rather like french-polished furniture. To see this splendid tree gleaming in the winter is a joy indeed. Avoid buying a weeping form of this tree which has been grafted — the weeping branches disguise the trunk. Whether you use birches, this cherry, one of the snake and paper-barked maples such as *Acer griseum* and *A. pennsylvanicum*, or any other tree with beautiful bark, do consider planting all such trees in multiples. This will effectively compound the result you are seeking. Be aware, though, that not all trees form good groups; the shape of an individual tree in itself may be desirable, and would be disguised in group plantings.

As young leaves can produce effects with their different hues, so too can young bark appear in shades not seen in older wood. It is therefore a good idea to try to rejuvenate

ABOVE: So many of the plants of the cottage garden have exquisite scents. They suit the informal garden with all of its romantic implications.

plants that have this feature, to ensure young bark is consistently produced.

Before discussing some of the plants for which rejuvenating bark is advisable, we should look at the problems associated with this technique. The greatest is the gap left in planting when the pruning is complete. This problem will arise when plants are cut back to their stems, but also arises when plants are cut back for foliage or simply to be rejuvenated.

How can this problem be addressed? One secret is to use an effective plant in front that will grow quickly in spring to cover the hole. Many of the deciduous herbaceous plants, such as the rudbeckias, can achieve this effectively. Remember that these decorative barks are most useful in the winter when many other plants are dormant, so that pruning them in spring is most beneficial. They will regrow through the summer for display next winter.

Given the space restrictions of the small garden, you will not want to use too many plants that require pruning to maximize their effect — the gaps would be too obvious. You might find space for *Cornus alba* 'Sibirica' or *C. stolonifera* 'Flaviramea', which can be grown as an attractive group. Prune them every two years to get the best from them and place them where they can be reflected in water.

FRUIT-BEARING PLANTS

Fruit, too, is a most valuable part of the smaller garden. This is partly because of the decorative quality of fruit trees, but also because they can be used to attract native birds and animals. To encourage these visitors to your garden you might think about concentrating on local species of berry-producing plants. Birds, with their high mobility, will be especially able to prosper from your generosity. The fruit-bearing trees act as a food supply and prevent the birds' dependence on humans.

As far as ornamental fruits are concerned, use plants that hold their fruit for a long time rather than dropping them quickly. The range of plants that offer this quality is extensive. Persimmons, for example, offer exquisite foliage shades, while the large golden orbs of fruit hang for long periods on the tree like so many lanterns. Of the crab-apples, I would choose the cultivar 'John Downie', because it holds its splendid, orange-fleshed, slightly astringent fruit for so long into the fall (autumn). Not far behind in quality is the delightful *Malus* 'Golden Hornet', again holding its fruit long; eventually the ground will be covered with fallen fruit as if there had been a golden hailstorm. There is also the *M. hupehensis,* with its tiny fruit blushing red where they face the sun. Berries or fruit are produced by so many plants — the pyracanthas, cotoneasters, apples, barberries, mahonias, and amelanchiers. Indeed, plants of such a diversity are available that it is almost impossible to create a garden without selecting at least a few good berrying plants.

Avoid sterile forms if you can. Such plants do not produce fruit, and this is a constant disappointment. The seed heads of smaller plants can be highly ornamental. The silvery moon seed heads of honesty (*Lunaria annua*), the heads of teazels (*Dipsacus sylvestris)* or the stems and seed heads of many grasses can all add outstanding winter value when leaves have fallen and there may be little flower display.

PLANTS TO ADD LAYERS

Overcoming the dullness of winter is never easy. I like to choose plants that fill gaps left by others, and I try to plant in layers to give the greatest chance of achieving some form of year-round cover. This approach to planting is a simple one, and will encourage you to think in three-dimensional terms. A plan may often appear full, whereas in fact there are gaps beneath trees and shrubs. By considering planting in layers, we are able to dictate the effects we want. In some instances we may wish to screen fences, however, and "borrow" a tree from next door. No tree layer would be required in this type of garden, but then the shrub layer becomes vital, with ground-covers beneath.

Layers offer us the greatest potential and interest when designing small gardens. The first layer is the ground-cover layer, for it is this which holds together our planting, linking separate shrubs or herbaceous plants, just like a carpet or rug covers the floor of our house and links seats and tables. Plant ground-covers especially in large groups and, as far as it is practicable, use evergreen species.

Another group with great value is the group of emergent plants, plants that rise from the ground-covering plant mass to give a vertical thrust to design. These can be repeated and spread through a piece of planting to give a link on another dimension from that of the ground-cover plants. Grasses and sedges work especially well in this context, as do many of the bulbs, such as species *Gladiolus,* though some of these may perform in a seasonal way, offering a short display before disappearing again. They can be naturalized, however, which is a great advantage when you want to achieve a striking garden with minimum effort.

ARCHITECTURAL & DECORATIVE FEATURES

Features for style

Small gardens do not need too many features. With only limited space available, there is a great danger of visual conflict between the different elements of the site. My best advice is to keep these elements simple and therefore more effective.

Most particularly, features added to a garden should underline and enhance the style of garden you have chosen to pursue. Cottage gardens, for example, require a simple and unsophisticated approach, so the addition of a feature such as a highly designed seat would be sadly out of place here. It is vital to make careful decisions about such features; if you do not see exactly what you want in your local garden store, wait until you find the perfect solution.

WATER

Water is a wonderful adjunct to any garden. In a small garden there is unlikely to be sufficient space for informal water, such as a cascading waterfall, so a formal pond, square, rectangular or circular, will be more suitable. Place it so that it may be seen from a dining-room or living-room, and use lighting so that it becomes an evening feature. Sun is also vital if water is to look its best, so place your pond where water droplets from a fountain, lit by sunlight, can look like diamonds.

People are drawn to water, so have it where it can be accessed easily, and if you really want it to be enjoyed, build a wall around the pond or pool at sitting level, so that people can sit and run their fingers

ABOVE: Well-chosen garden furniture can provide an extra dimension to a small garden. Difficult to conceal, it can be made a bold feature of a garden. This seat is not only a decorative feature providing charm and focus but also creates a welcoming corner in the garden.

OPPOSITE: Well-designed features add particular qualities to a garden but there should not be too many so that they conflict with each other, and most importantly they should suit the style of the garden.

PREVIOUS PAGE: Decorative features such as birdbaths become a focal point in a small garden and it is important that they are not in competition with other potential focuses. Mass planting of scented herbs, lavenders and perennials provides a soft complement.

through it. This can help keep pets and children out too. Where a pond is an integral part of a paved area, raise its edge slightly so that chairs, for example, do not fall into it. Also ensure that the dimensions of the pond reflect the dimensions of the paving. Add brightness to the garden by using tiles to line the pond, and keep the water and pond base clean so the tiles look their best. Water looks especially good when it reflects boldly foliaged plants or has an attractive clump of foliage growing out of it, so try to make the most of any pond by arranging your planting successfully.

Wall fountains are a great attraction; they combine the qualities of fountains with elements of sculpture. I prefer French enamel fountains, made to fit against a wall, to lion heads, because they are so much bigger. There is no doubt, however, that whichever you choose you will be able to bring life and movement to a garden at the flick of a switch.

SCULPTURE

Statues can be difficult to use in a garden, not least because so many of them are reproductions of well-known figures or coy and romantic images. I prefer to avoid these and use a piece of contemporary work, which will look more original. The great value of such features is their ability to create a change in texture in a garden; ceramics, stone and concrete can all achieve this. Grow foliage across and around your sculpture to ensure that you achieve maximum impact and make it part of the garden.

Where large sculptures are placed against climbing plants, incorporate them into the garden by allowing the climber to festoon the sculpture, but not to the extent that the sculpture is hidden. Use the principle of "enough and not too much"; use your eye to get the balance right.

I view sundials, birdbaths, and even strongly shaped urns and pots as pieces of sculpture. The potential for their use is considerable, but do realize that each of these items will be focal points. By using them you are inviting the garden viewer to look at them. They should therefore be a focus to a scene and should not conflict with other potential focuses. This placement becomes all important, either on a central axis, for example where one walks up a set of formal stairs and straight along a path to a terminal focus or as a feature in an asymmetrical garden where the eye is carried across a diagonal to achieve an effect of size and distance.

Any of these features can also be used to provide charm, or a focus for a small spot. Ensure that you place them in a setting suitable for their scale; for example, a sculpture placed against a dominant party wall will appear totally inadequate. Cover this type of wall with lattice and a climber and create a niche suitable for the sculpture, and the whole feel of the garden will change; also, the sculpture will now be in scale with its setting. Used well, an element of this type can be lit so that when visible from a window it changes the quality of a view.

In all designs it is worth ensuring that placement ensures a focus. You might use two ball decorations at the top of steps to frame them. Steps also frame a view, and could lead the eye to a seat or tree or other focus. The use of two features side by side is usually uncomfortable for the eye, and

ABOVE: Containers play an integral part in this highly formal design.

creates an unresolved quality. A similar condition occurs when plants are grouped in even numbers. Also, trees should be planted in odd numbers, unless they line a path, in which case a focus such as a fountain may be needed at the end. An avenue of trees is not, however, a likely design proposal for a small garden, where there may only be sufficient space for one or two trees at most.

CONTAINERS

The use of containers can add enormously to the style and mood of a garden. The fact that they can be moved about is of immense value, since it means you have more flexibility. You could stand the containers around an outdoor eating area and then move them next to the front door if your needs change. For flexibility of positioning, choose lightweight containers. Plastic tubs need not be too gaudy these days. There are beautiful inexpensive ones based on classical shapes, and because they are not porous like terracotta, the plants in them require less frequent watering; evaporation loss is also reduced. However, terracotta pots achieve a lovely patina and are available in a range of shapes and sizes. There are also numerous forms of glazed pots, decorative in their own right. When selecting, remember that their fundamental role is to provide a home for decorative plants and not to steal the show themselves.

Containers enable you to establish central points of colour, or of formality. Annual display plants in various tones are always attractive to the eye and can be altered cheaply and seasonally to give three or four different schemes a year. Use some key foliage plants for continuity. For example, the silver-leaved *Helichrysum petiolare* is always a popular choice, though

ABOVE: Arches, trellis and furniture are all useful garden features. Ensure that they suit the style of the garden. Much of the style of an arbour results from the plants grown over it while if sufficiently large they can offer effective shade in summer for sitting outside.

surprisingly intolerant of dryness, while olives, cumquats or clipped bay and box are larger, but excellent, permanent foliage plants. Bulbs offer great winter display, but replace them quickly before they become dowdy with plants for summer brightness. Use some plants to tumble over the edge of your containers to soften them.

Use a commercial potting mix in containers, and avoid putting gravel in the base of your pots. This often leads to a reduction in the effective rooting volume of the pot, which is especially critical where shallow pots are concerned.

A few well-planted containers will look better than a plethora of different sized pots, and nothing looks worse than pots of half-dead plants. Not all containers in one group need be of a consistent size, nor need they all be planted alike. I enjoy having a permanent planted element while changing other plantings, but do link your pot group in some way. For example, use white impatiens as a bedding display in all of your pots, in conjunction with various other plants. In small gardens, avoid having containers overwhelm your site, but do enjoy them, as they are an invaluable part of the garden.

Window boxes can be especially effective for herbs, or to brighten a bleak view, especially in winter. Set outside the kitchen window, basil, parsley and sage grow if there is sufficient sun, while some crocuses offer winter cheer in their season.

ARCHES AND FRAMES

The framing effect achieved by an avenue of trees on a large site may be achieved by arches or small pergolas in the smaller garden. Their presence will hold the eye within a view, leading it in a logical progression to a terminal focus.

Arches may be made of many materials. A do-it-yourselfer may choose timber. Ensure that it is dressed, chamfer the corners and think about the way a corner bracket might help to produce both stability and a design motif that will give cohesion to your site. You may, for example, repeat a motif from your house, or use this motif in a pergola. Paint or treat all cut areas with preservative to prevent decay. You may be best advised to use stirrup cups to keep the timber off the ground.

Metal arches are popular. They can be very plain, created purely from bent metal, or more complex, with decorative treatment to suit a cottage style. Ask yourself whether you want to enjoy the plants or the arch. If the former, select a simple arch that allows the plants to show themselves off; if the latter, select a decorative arch and keep climbing plants thinned out. In most cases the first option is preferable.

Use arches to frame viewlines and path lines, especially where you want to contain the view. By extending their form you could make a simple cross structure at the crossing point of a path. Do remember just how voluminous the growth of climbers can be, and ensure that you make your arches sufficiently high for both this growth and for people passing through them; there is always the temptation to reduce the height of what appear to be unrealistically high arches only to find that they have become too low when the climber prospers.

A slightly different concept is the use of a series of timber or masonry frames like a series of picture frames. These can create a charming effect if climbing plants are trained over them and there is good planting behind: almost like looking through a series of picture frames at the garden beyond. To create further separation, you could use a low wall as a base to these frames to permit sitting, or, more interesting perhaps, you could make this wall a planter box, in which an upward-thrusting small plant such as English lavender (*Lavandula angustifolia*) can look superb, especially if climbing roses hang down from above. This type of separation, where there is a functional separation of space but still visual continuity, is ideal for small gardens.

PERGOLAS

Pergolas work best if they are linked to the house. Their shade can be especially useful if the sun should be too hot in summer. Designed properly — using an architect will help — they can be built to permit spring, fall (autumn) and winter sun to enter while screening the worst summer rays. Pergolas can also provide privacy,, especially if used in conjunction with climbing plants.

Pergolas are generally made of timber, and look best if painted the same shade as the woodwork of the house. Judging the size of them can be difficult; if they are too small they will not provide adequate shade, and if they are too large they can restrict the open space of the garden. Design them to accommodate a table and chairs for outdoor eating, and always soften them with planting to remove their naked quality.

Pergolas can also be used in separate decking areas on sloping sites, or perhaps in a paved sitting area specifically located to obtain sun. They might also be used beside a swimming pool. In each of these cases there may be an opportunity to create and define a very clear space, with the pergola structure separate from the rest of the garden. Extend the space with low fencing, and you can create a suitable fence for your swimming pool as an integral protection. The more ambitious your design, however, the more expensive such a feature becomes, and the more difficult it will be for the do-it-yourselfer to make.

GAZEBOS

In its sophisticated form the pergola becomes a gazebo, though this is generally more elaborate and expensive than a pergola. Do ensure that a gazebo does not overwhelm the whole of your garden. Remember you have a limited space, and this space will appear larger if the structures in it are refined, elegant and simple rather than being too fussy.

Gazebos come in many shapes and sizes. They may be small timber shelters like sophisticated sheds, designed to create an outdoor room where you might sit and read. These shelters may even be connected to your electricity supply, so that you can sit outside well into winter.

Build your gazebo in conjunction with suitable paving to establish a setting, and make the garden here a little more formal, no matter how informal its overall effect. Site the gazebo in such a way that it provides the type of facility you require. If much of your yard is shaded, and so the gazebo is not required merely for shade, place the gazebo with its surrounding planting so as to create privacy, a place where you can sit and entertain. Always remember that if you intend to use it as an eating area, you will need clear access from your kitchen.

A gazebo will inevitably provide a focus to the garden. Plan your site to incorporate it effectively, and make sure it fits the context of the site. If your home has the feel of a cottage, then give the gazebo a rustic air. A more formal house demands a more formal gazebo.

FENCES

Fences are a garden structure I especially like to use. One of the ways to increase the apparent size of a small garden is to divide it up. Then there will be a cumulative effect of greater size as the eye puts the "blocks" together to create a whole. Simple fences can do this quite effectively. Choose a style of fencing that suits your garden. Picket fences, for example, would be fine for a cottage garden. Division will be achieved by a fence about 6ft (1.8m) high. Patterned open fences give a more traditional approach. I especially like their use between patios and other garden areas. Always use them as a climbing frame for plants. Fences with climbers are generally more desirable in small gardens than hedges, because they take up less space.

ABOVE: A gazebo is an effective feature where space allows. Placed too close to a house, there can be a conflict between the two architectures, but in this location the gazebo offers an alternative micro-climate in the garden, giving a shaded sitting area where the rest of the garden is fully exposed to the sun. Do attempt to relate the design of the gazebo to the style of the house.

CREATING LEVELS

The challenge of slopes

Sloping gardens are among the most difficult to design. A small garden with a slope towards the house will appear smaller than it really is, and will tend to feel enclosed. This effect will be worsened by the use of tall trees or a large gazebo at the end of the garden, for these will appear to be tumbling down the slope towards the house. This is an unattractive feature, and creates an uncomfortable feeling. Good planning can do much to overcome this situation.

A slope away from the house is preferable, since it can open up the opportunity for views, and though your own space may be small the effect will be one of extended spaciousness. It may be that some elements of the view are unattractive and that others

OPPOSITE: Changes in level give an excellent opportunity to use water. The sound of it in movement gives a special appeal to any garden. The line of the path is delineated by white timber frames providing a strong terminal element to the design as well as an ideal place to grow some delightful climbers.

PREVIOUS PAGE: This splendid garden is full of character. The simple wide steps allow the character of the wellhead to be fully appreciated while the masses of plants are strong and effective. The vibrant mauve Geranium psilostemon, *the silver foliage of* Pyrus salicifolia 'Pendula', *and the blue heads of agapanthus especially form a most exciting combination.*

offer fine scenery. The use of screening plants becomes important here, though the limited space available for their planting may restrict just what you can use. Screening does not imply that a dense, full screen needs to be established. Quite often breaking up the outline of the offending structure, for example a rooftop or adjacent building, will be sufficient to achieve an improved view. The danger of a very strong screen is that it will achieve the opposite effect to that required: it may draw attention to the fact that an unsightly view is being screened. A lot can be achieved by a single tree, if it is well placed.

The fact that there is an "away" slope in one part of the site often suggests that there is an opposite slope in the other part. Slopes toward the house give a sense of reduced spaciousness. Little can be done to overcome this effect completely, but there are a few golden rules.

THE USE OF TERRACES
Create a good terrace against the house. This creates level and usable areas and will establish a sense of space against the windows and doors. Whether at the front or rear of the house, it will be a useful functional space. At the front the terrace may permit a formal entrance area, where paving and a few pots offer a setting for welcoming and farewelling guests. A terrace at the rear may allow an outdoor sitting area; this could be very shady if facing away from the sun, but delightfully sunny and warm if facing the

sun, and quite possibly very private. Terraces may not be very wide, but they can provide areas for sitting, pattern gardens, ponds or lawns, and generally they offer easier maintenance than a slope.

The disadvantage of terraces is the construction cost; this could be quite considerable because of the need to build retaining walls and steps. But terraces do not always have to be made with retaining walls; they can be made of timber, in the form of decking linked by steps or boardwalks. In a small garden with fine views, such a treatment can give wonderful results, offering a complete living area not otherwise available where there are steep slopes! If you have significant drops from decking or terraces you will need to have a simple safety rail added to save people from falling over.

Design timber deckings to establish a system of usable garden spaces, interspersed with effective plantings. The decking areas are best if sufficiently tall to create isolated spaces. Deckings are especially useful around swimming pools and spas on steep slopes, since they overcome the need for very large retaining walls. Space beneath decking can in some cases be useful storage space, and the deck may even form the cover of a carport.

Try to keep your timber off the ground, for example by using concrete footings to prevent rotting, and ensure that where containers are being used they can be easily moved and that water is contained rather than pouring onto the wood.

STEPS

Steps can be exciting elements of a garden. Ensure they are consistently dimensioned in any single flight. On gentle slopes they can have a shallow angle and deep treads, creating a leisurely mood well suited to a garden, whereas on steep slopes they should be steeper, with shallower treads. The design of the steps will dictate much of the mood of the garden; they could, for example, be wide and have tubs or pots on either side to give formality and display. In contrast, they may be quite informal, made of rock, and winding their way down a hillside to create a natural informal effect. Never forget that steps establish the direction in which users will look and in which they will set off once they reach the base; as their designer, you can dictate much of the way your garden works by ensuring that movement is in the direction you want it to be.

ABOVE: Terraces falling away from the house allow a view down into the site where pattern can be especially attractive. Subtle changes in shadow have special appeal where the light is strong while from a practical viewpoint shadows provide an opportunity to retreat from the full intensity of the sun.

PLANTING TO PREVENT EROSION

On sloping sites, one of the major concerns is to avoid erosion. The use of terraces with effective drainage behind retaining walls can help, but the construction of terraces is not always either feasible or practical. The use of plants to reduce erosion then becomes important. Choose plants with a fibrous root system, for example the dwarf mountain pine (*Pinus mugo*), or a plant that suckers and thus completely covers the ground. *Rosa rugosa* would do this superbly, and also offer a dense and beautiful cover with excellent foliage, fruit, and flowers. Select evergreen plants where possible, making up several layers of foliage cover to impede the speed of raindrops and thus reduce their damaging impact at ground level. Mulches, too, are important. A layer of organic material is generally quickly absorbent of water, reducing run-off and thus erosion.

RETAINING WALLS

If you use retaining walls, have them professionally designed by an engineer, since these walls may be holding back considerable loads of soil and ground-water and perhaps the pressures created by sizeable tree roots. In combination, this can soon lead to the wall being over-turned.

Retaining walls can be very strong elements in a garden and look very harsh. They may not look too bad if the slope falls away from your vision, but those which are part of the view should be screened. Some, like crib walls, contain pockets for filling with plants, and these walls may be almost totally hidden once the pockets are filled with species such as *Cotoneaster* 'Skogholm' or *C. dammeri*, or one of the low-growing junipers, such as *Juniperus horizontalis*.

In these circumstances, a wall of green may be sufficient. Where display is required, there are numerous ornamental flowering plants able to tolerate these conditions, given sufficient sun. Foremost among these is *Convolvulus mauretanicus*, with its exquisite blue flowers against its silvery foliage, or the Mexican daisy (*Erigeron mucronatus*), a delightful rambler, able to succeed in most sunny places.

More structured and formal retaining walls give less opportunity to interplant, though you may be able to design them to give you planting opportunities, by omitting the occasional brick or creating a specific planting niche. Look to those plants that naturally inhabit rocky hillsides to colonize these niches. The red valerian (*Centranthus ruber*) will do so, but may reach plague proportions. The Kenilworth ivy (*Cymbalaria muralis*) is good in this situation, and beautifully delicate. Where there are no toe-holds for covering plants to grow from, allow climbers to tumble over your retaining walls. Clematis will do so delightfully, and can make a daring combination with plants growing up from below. Alternatively, use evergreen shrubs across the wall to soften its face. These could even be clipped hard, like hedges. The lovely small-leaved euonymuses and pyracantha with its fierce berries are outstanding in these circumstances.

You can also soften the effect of retaining walls by using them as a basis for raised beds. This treatment is especially useful for people with restricted mobility or disabilities, or for older people for whom bending may be a problem. With raised beds, plants are brought closer to the eye, inviting our inspection of them, so use plants with excellent texture,

especially if you can have them spilling over the edge and they can contrast with the masonry. Ensure the masonry of the walls relates to the materials of your house, and ensure that you install effective drainage, for the health of your plants and to reduce the load on your walls. Add water in a rectangular or square pond to bring life to this type of design.

Gravels are not needed at the base of containers created from part of a retaining wall. Rather use a mesh over drains to prevent loss of fine material, and use a commercially available, growing medium rather than ordinary garden soil. These growing media are specially prepared for this type of use, and provide a good air-to-water ratio to encourage effective root growth and good drainage. Because they are made largely of organic materials, they do break down over time, and you will need to top them up periodically.

ABOVE: Brick is a dominant texture in this scheme, in the wall and retaining wall. Bricks offer an effective foil for plants, in this case Hedera helix *'Buttercup',* Euphorbia melliflora, *and the white flowered* Choisya ternata.

PLANTS FOR THE SMALL GARDEN

Choosing plants

Before deciding on the plants you will grow in your small garden, try to view them in a mature garden so that you can gain a sense of their eventual size. Also remember that you need not allow plants to grow to their full size and maturity, for they may be too large for your garden when they reach this stage. Trees often create this problem. Rather treat your plants in a dynamic way, removing them as they become too large or pruning them as this becomes necessary to keep them in shape. You will find that the division of perennial plants is a vital process for retaining their sturdiness. The spare pieces will make excellent gifts, but avoid distributing those that have been weedy for you.

Ensure that the plants you select suit your growing conditions. To do this, look at nearby gardens or local parks for growing examples. If you cannot find any, your local nursery will be able to give you good advice about the plants you want. If these are not suited to your location, the nursery will be able to suggest alternatives for you to consider.

Never forget that the better suited any chosen plant is to your garden conditions, the better it will grow. This means there will be fewer problems with disease, a healthier appearance and less demand for maintenance. While you may see your small garden as being small enough to look after easily, you will find that plants requiring low maintenance will give you more time for enjoying your garden.

Remember that the plant groupings referred to in books have been determined by human decisions, and that in nature there are no such categories or groupings. Exactly what is a tree and what is a shrub is not easy to say; we are often able to provide an input into gardens that allows us to control the eventual form of a plant. Take for example *Camellia sasanqua*, which when unconfined will grow to a large shrub. Given suitable training this splendid plant can grow as a wall-hugging hedge, a perfect screen in a small garden. Active control of plants becomes especially important in small gardens, where no plants can be allowed to grow out of their allotted space.

With trees, consider the type of shade the tree may produce, as light shade is often especially welcome in the small garden, as it retains good light access but offers protection as well.

OPPOSITE: Crush planting achieves a lush effect and allows relationships between flowers to be fully developed. Geranium pratense, G. macrorrhizum, *and astrantia provide a background for the magenta spears of* Gladiolus communis *ssp.* byzantinus, *always a focus wherever it is used.*

PREVIOUS PAGE: House and garden should be viewed as a unit. Bright and cheerful paintwork is reflected in bright planting: yellows, blues, oranges and whites combining to give a flamboyant and eye-catching effect.

PLANT SELECTION LISTS

Plants identified in the following lists may fit several categories. There may, for example, be an evergreen ground-cover with excellent textural qualities.

DECIDUOUS TREES

Acer
Maples

Many maples suit the small garden. Generally their flowers are small and relatively insignificant, so choose those with attractive foliage and effective bark display. *Acer griseum* (paper-bark maple) grows to 40ft (12m) high and 30ft (9m) wide, has peeling coppery brown bark, and is especially effective when grouped. Low germination rates make this an expensive choice (Zone 5-8). *A. rufinerve* (grey-budded snake-bark maple) grows to 30ft (9m) high, 20ft (6m) wide, has green bark with greyish white vertical stripes (Zone 4-6). *A. buergerianum* (trident maple), 25ft (7.5m) high, 20ft (6m) wide, has a shaggy bark and a three-pointed leaf, giving fall (autumn) shades from orange through red to cochineal (Zone 6-8).

Japanese maple *A. japonicum* 'Aureum', 15ft (4.5m) high, 12ft (3.5m) wide, has yellow foliage, and the cultivar 'Vitifolium', 20ft (6m) high and wide, provides brilliant fall (autumn) reds. Of *A. palmatum* cultivars, many are shrubs, but there are fine smaller trees: 'Atropurpureum', 15ft (4.5m) high and wide with purple foliage, 'Osakazuki',

10ft (3m) high, 12ft (3.5m) wide with blazing scarlet fall (autumn) foliage, and 'Senkaki', 20ft (6m) high, 15ft (4.5m) wide with coral-pink young bark. Maples are undemanding, needing a rich moist soil and not dense shade. Best fall (autumn) shades are achieved where temperatures are low.

Aesculus
Horse chestnuts, buckeye

Many of this genus become too large for the small garden. *Aesculus glabra* (Ohio buckeye), to 30ft (9m) high and wide, would make a good choice for a specimen tree on an open lawn. Low-branching with greyish white spikes of flowers and yellow fall (autumn) foliage. Enjoys moist, well-drained soil (Zone 4).

Albizia
Silk tree

Albizia julibrissin offers delectable shade, and forms a tree 30ft (9m) high, 25ft (7.5m) wide. Fern-like, feathery foliage offers a delightful cap to a paved terrace. Brittle wood may lead to loss of branches. Suits an open, well-drained soil. Light pinky mauve flowers, as delicate as the leaves, and a fine complement to them (Zone 7).

Amelanchier
Serviceberry, snowy mespilus

Serviceberries are ideal small garden trees and shrubs, perfect in size, with good flower, foliage, and fruit and an excellent tolerance of soil types, except those too dry or waterlogged. *Amelanchier lamarckii,* 30ft (9m) high, 15ft (4.5m) wide, produces a suckering small tree with graceful branches, and pure white flowers, when the young leaves retain their bronze tinting. Purple-black berries are sweet and succulent to eat, providing you get to them before the birds

do. Good fall (autumn) tints of yellows and bronze (Zone 5).

Betula
Birch

Birches are popular trees for small gardens with their graceful branches and white trunks. Especially effective en masse and can be grown as multi-stemmed trees by placing several young seedlings in a single planting hole.

Betula papyrifera (paper birch), 70ft (21.5m) high, 30ft (9m) wide, is tolerant of moist soils, and produces one of the whitest of birch trunks (Zone 2). *B. pendula* (European birch) is a slightly weeping form best in the cultivar 'Tristis', 50ft (15m) high, 20ft (6m) wide. *B. pendula* 'Fastigiata' can be useful in narrow spaces, for example to separate a pedestrian entrance from a driveway (Zone 2). Birches are tolerant of various soils but dislike drying out and are intolerant of shade.

Cercidyphyllum
Katsura tree

Cercidyphyllum japonicum, large for the small garden when mature, 60ft (18m) high, 40ft (12m) wide, possesses an attractively layered form, with delightfully textured leaves giving medium shade density and good fall (autumn) hues. Resistant to diseases and pests but dislikes waterlogging (Zone 5).

Cercis
Redbud, Judas tree, rosebud,

Cercis canadensis (redbud), 35ft (10.5m) high, 30ft (9m) wide, and *C. siliquastrum* (Judas tree), 25ft (7.5m) high, 20ft (6m) wide, both provide heart-shaped foliage fluttering in the wind and pea flowers in shades from purple-pink to white, early in

spring before leaves develop. When growing and flowering well they give the effect of a mauvy haze in the garden. Flowers of *C. siliquastrum* are sweet and can be used in salads (Zone 5).

Carpinus
Hornbeam

Too large for small gardens if allowed to grow freely, *Carpinus betulus* makes an effective clipped hedge. It holds matt brown leaves throughout the winter. The cultivar 'Fastigiata' can provide sentinels to 40ft (12m) in a design, for example among loose plantings or to frame a pathway. Clip it to keep it tightly shaped and shorter. Good for open, well-drained soils (Zone 5).

Chionanthus
Fringe tree

Chionanthus virginicus looks like a snowstorm in late spring or early summer, when it is covered by a profusion of pendant white flowers. It produces light shade and golden fall (autumn) foliage, but may be slow-growing. Establish a thicket to enjoy its profuse display. Reaches 30ft (9m) high, 15ft (4.5m) wide. Enjoys moist, well-drained soils (Zone 5).

Cornus
Dogwood

Dogwoods are popular trees for small gardens and have many useful qualities. Identify those particularly suited to your area. *Cornus florida* (flowering dogwood) grows 30ft (9m) high, 20ft (6m) wide. It produces attractive fall (autumn) tints in oranges and reds but is grown for its spring bracts, varying from pinks through to white. Look out for selected cultivars 'Cherokee Chief' with rich ruby-red bracts

ABOVE: Trees provide a most effective ceiling to a space. The contrast between the yellow foliage of the golden robinia, Robinia pseudoacacia *'Frisia', and the dark green foliage of yew,* Taxus baccata, *is very strong, while the delicate shade of the golden robinia is the perfect place to sit.*

and 'White Cloud' with creamy white bracts (Zone 5). A hybrid with *C. nuttallii,* Pacific dogwood, known as 'Eddie's White Wonder', is a fine alternative. *C. kousa* var. *chinensis* to 25ft (7.5m) high, 20ft (6m) wide is excellent, offering fall (autumn) tints and a profusion of large white bracts (Zone 6). *C. controversa* 'Variegata' has layered, slender branches bearing variegated leaves, best displayed against a dark green, evergreen backdrop. It reaches 40ft (12m) high, 20ft (6m) wide (Zone 5). Dogwoods prefer moist but well-drained soils and perform best where they obtain some sun.

Crataegus
Hawthorn

Selecting the best from this highly decorative genus of plants depends upon whether flower, fruit, or foliage display is most important. Thorns can be a useful feature where security is important, but disadvantagous for young children. *Crataegus crus-galli,* cockspur thorn, 15ft (4.5m) high, 15ft (4.5m) wide, produces abundant flowers, brilliant scarlet autumn hues, and persistent large fruit (Zone 5). It is coarser than *C. phaenopyrum* (Washington

thorn), 25ft (7.5m) high, 20ft (6m) wide, notable for its lustrous green foliage and long-lasting scarlet berries (Zone 5). These two species bear large thorns in contrast to *C. tanacetifolia*, 35ft (10.5m) high, 20ft (6m) wide, with greyish leaves and yellow suffused large red fruit (Zone 5). One of the great qualities of hawthorns is that they attract birds to their prolific fruit. Few tree groups are more tolerant to diverse soil types and city pollution.

Ficus
Fig

Most figs are tropical or sub-tropical, but *Ficus carica*, the edible fig, is widely cultivated, tolerating some cold but being cut back by heavy frost. Where frosts are likely, grow it against a sunny wall. It is a small tree, 20ft (6m) high, 30ft (9m) wide, with bold foliage and good fruit, as long as soils are not too rich (Zone 7).

Ginkgo
Maidenhair tree

Ginkgo biloba has characteristic leaves and will ultimately become too large for the smallest gardens. Up to 80ft (24.5m) tall, it is a slow grower. It has a narrow form but produces random stiff, upward-growing branches. Avoid waterlogged soils, but it tolerates industrial and urban pollution. Superb bright butter-yellow fall (autumn) display. Avoid the female form, which produces malodourous fruit. Can be espaliered against walls, where its superbly textured leaves offer a fine contrast to masonry (Zone 5).

Halesia
Snowdrop tree

The white bell-shaped flowers of *Halesia carolina* (snowdrop tree) hang in plentiful display. It forms a small, to 25ft (7.5m), multi-stemmed tree, preferring acidic, well-drained loamy soils and a position sheltered from direct sun (Zone 5).

Kolreuteria
Golden rain tree

Kolreuteria paniculata (golden rain tree) is a lovely tree to 30ft (9m) high, 15ft (4.5m) wide, with good tolerance to pollution and a wide range of soils but not waterlogging. It has delightful foliage, the long leaves being divided into numerous leaflets to create a fern-like effect. It provides delicate shade, large panicles of massed yellow flowers especially prolific in sun, and black seeds in papery seed pods, but is not notable for its fall (autumn) display. It would be perfect in the corner of a small, walled front garden with lots of sun (Zone 6).

Lagerstroemia
Crepe myrtle

The crepe myrtle is notable for its smooth, undulating grey and olive green trunk, delicate foliage turning yellow in fall (autumn) and heads of flowers from white to deep red on different plants. It enjoys sun and can be grown in large containers or as a massed plant in formal arrangements, for example growing out of gravel. Can be prone to mildew. It reaches 20ft (6m) high, 15ft (4.5m) wide. Provide soils with good drainage (Zone 7).

Magnolia

Magnolias are fine garden plants, several having exquisite large, scented flowers and many superb large leaves, but others can be dull when not flowering. *Magnolia* x *soulangeana* is a variable, open tree to 20ft (6m), bearing low branches and goblet-shaped flowers stained with purple on the outside. Choose the cultivars 'Lennei Alba' and 'Brozzonii '. Does well in sun, in moist well-drained soil (Zone 6).

M. wilsonii and *M. sinensis* are similar, and in flower are one of the most marvellous sights. Pure white cup-shaped pendulous flowers have long rich red stamens. *M. wilsonii*, 25ft (7.5m) high, is said to be less spreading than *M. sinensis* and so finer for the small garden but either would be outstanding (Zone 6).

Malus
Crab-apple

Do not ignore the quality of fruiting apple trees for small gardens, especially the dwarf forms now available. Some are especially good in containers. The crab-apples offer useful fruit and a most decorative plant group for small gardens. Choose from those with purple or green foliage, usable fruit, or dramatic floral display. Visit local gardens to view and select from the many forms. Particularly good species include *Malus ioensis* (Bechtel crab), 20ft (6m) high, 12ft (3.5m) wide, with sumptuous rich creamy pink flowers and attractive golden fall (autumn) foliage (Zone 6), and *M. hupehensis*, 40ft (12m) high, 20ft (6m) wide, stiff branching with flowers, reddish pink in bud, opening white or pink. Small red fruit hang on the tree into winter (Zone 4).

M. floribunda becomes tangled as it ages, but produces masses of rosy red and pink flowers on a tree 30ft (9m) high and wide. Among those producing the most ornamental crab-apples are 'John Downie', 25ft (7.5m) high, 20ft (6m) wide, with profuse clusters of bright orange and scarlet, tangy to eat and remaining on the tree (Zone 5). 'Golden Hornet', 20ft (6m) high and wide, with deep yellow fruit, is profuse and lasting. Also try 'Gorgeous', with glossy red cherry-like fruit (Zone 6).

Purple-leaved apples can appear dull and drear, and do little to enliven a shaded garden. Crab-apples do best in rich, well-drained soils.

Melia
White cedar, chinaberry

Excellent where rapid cover is required. *Melia azederach*, 45ft (15m) high, 30ft (9m) wide, produces fragrant silvery-mauve flowers and light shade. Its numerous small orangey brown fruit are poisonous and messy when they are shed. Useful for shade on a patio (Zone 7).

Nothofagus
Southern beech

Fine leaves and a layered branch form make the southern beeches attractive. Mature specimens of many of these trees will be too large for smaller gardens but their generally slow growth rates makes them very useful. The most suitable is *Nothofagus antarctica*, 40ft (12m) high, 20ft (6m) wide, with long, elegant branches arranged in one plane, providing a most graceful effect. Useful as a screen because of its low-branching character. It performs best in a sunny location, but is quite tolerant of soil types (Zone 2).

Prunus

Few genera provide as much flower variation and interest as *Prunus,* which includes apricots, cherries, plums, peaches and almonds. Many of the fruiting forms can be effective, contributing attractive flowers and useful fruit, but there are many trees grown largely for ornamental quality. As with the crab-apples it is worth visiting display gardens to assess the quality of the different types available.

Among the most intense is the *Prunus campanulata* (bell-flowered cherry), 30ft

(9m) high, 30ft (9m) wide, with pendulous deep rose spring flowers (Zone 7). The flowers of *Prunus subhirtella* are soft rose. It is frequently cultivated as *P.s.* 'Pendula Rosea' or 'Pendula Rubra', two lovely weeping trees, but wide-spreading 'Autumnalis' flowers in both spring and fall (autumn) (Zone 6).

Prunus serrula (Tibetan cherry), 30ft (9m) high, 25ft (7.5m) wide, has willow-like leaves and bright, brown peeling bark, but small dull flowers. Avoid selecting a grafted tree with weeping branches, for these disguise the bark and largely nullify its quality (Zone 5).

Prunus serrulata is the commonest of garden cherries, grown in one of its many cultivars. 'Amanogawa' is narrow and upright, 'Kanzan', to 40ft (12m), is a sturdy form with double pink flowers, and 'Ukon', 25ft (7.5m) high and wide, is a vigorous tree with greenish yellow petals (Zone 6).

Cherries do not enjoy heavy or water-logged soils or pruning, being subject to disease.

Pyrus
Pear

A pear orchard in flower is a memorable sight, but pears are frequently overlooked when selecting trees for gardens. The popularity of the grey garden at Sissinghurst Castle has led to an increase in the use of *Pyrus salicifolia* (willow-leaved pear), 25ft (7.5m) high, 20ft (6m) wide, so that it is seen almost too frequently. It produces grey leaves and white flowers together in spring and is most commonly seen in its pendulous form (Zone 6).

Robinia
False acacia

Robinia pseudacacia (false acacia), 70ft (21.5m) high, 40ft (12m) wide, with feathery foliage, perfect to shade an outdoor eating terrace. Its white pea-like flowers are borne in racemes. Several forms are available. 'Frisia', with golden-yellow foliage, is one of the most popular. Limbs are easily broken in strong winds so plant in a sheltered position or choose a compact cultivar, for example 'Bessoniana'. Robinias grow best in well-drained soils and sunny locations (Zone 6).

Sorbus
Mountain ash

The mountain ash include fine trees with foliage displaying fall (autumn) hues and excellent textures. Many produce brilliant fruit too, berry-like, varying from white through yellow to orange and red. It is excellent in most soils as long as they are well drained. *Sorbus aucuparia* (mountain ash) is a lovely small tree, 30ft (9m) high, 20ft (6m) wide, prolific in flowers and fruit. Birds are attracted by the bright red fruit, and flocks raid the crop in fall (autumn) (Zone 5). The yellow-fruited *S.* 'Joseph Rock', 45ft (14m) high, 20ft (6m) wide, is one of the most magnificent small trees, the fruit contrasting with the crimson, purple, and scarlet hues of the fall (autumn) foliage (Zone 5).

S. aria (whitebeam), 50ft (15m) high, 30ft (91m) wide, has simple leaves in contrast to the pinnate leaves of the other species mentioned. Whitebeam is a fine tree, tolerant of coastal and industrial locations, with a silver underside to its leaves and huge crops of bright red fruit (Zone 4).

Stewartia

This supremely beautiful family of plants dislikes alkaline soils but thrives in moist acid soils protected from direct sun. The two most frequently available are *Stewartia pseudocamellia* (deciduous camellia), 35ft (10.5m) high, 15ft (4.5m) wide, and *S.*

pseudocamellia var. *koreana* of similar size. They are very alike, the former having more cupped flowers. These are similar to and related to camellias, with single white flowers. Equally attractive is the orange-brown bark, which becomes bright orange as the aged bark falls. Fall (autumn) tones are also superb, from yellow to dark red. Providing they can be found in a nursery, these will be among the loveliest of trees for the small garden (Zone 6).

Styrax
Snowbell tree

A graceful tree, *Styrax japonica* (snowbell tree), 25ft (7.5m) high, 15ft (4.5m) wide, makes a fine specimen in the small garden where soil is acid. It bears pendulous pure white flowers in summer (Zone 6).

Syringa
Lilac

Most lilacs are large shrubs rather than trees, though *Syringa reticulata* (Japanese tree lilac), 30ft (9m) high, 12ft (3.5m) wide, is useful for the small garden, retaining a columnar habit allowing light into the garden. In the middle of summer masses of white flowers with a rich purple-pink outside are produced if the tree is sited in full sun (Zone 5).

EVERGREEN TREES

Abies
Korean fir

A delightful fir, *Abies koreana*, 60ft (18m) high, 25ft (7.5m) wide, is eventually too large, but splendid while young, notably for its blue cones, borne even when the tree is small. Treat it as an ornamental feature tree and replace when too large for the garden. This tree dislikes dry or shallow soils.

Arbutus

Arbutuses are grown for the glossy evergreen foliage, pitcher-shaped flowers, strawberry-like fruit and attractive bark, bright red in the best specimens. *Arbutus unedo* (Irish strawberry tree), 30ft (9m) high, 20ft (6m) wide, forms a broadly crowned tree. *A. menziesii,* 60ft (18m) high, 30ft (9m) wide, native to California, is a noble and beautiful tree of a size that would require its use as a feature specimen in the small garden (Zone 8). A hybrid *A.* x *andrachioides* is an open-canopied tree with large flower truss size and remarkable branch tones.

Azara

Azaras are small trees ideally suited to the small garden because of their delicate foliage and scented small flowers. *Azara lanceolata* produces massed, petalless yellow flowers while *A. microphylla,* 20ft (6m) high, 5ft (1.5m) wide, has a fishbone branch form with a marked weeping and vanilla-scented creamy flowers. Both, but especially the latter, have a marked tolerance of shade (Zone 7).

Bauhinia
Butterfly tree

Bauhinia variegata (butterfly tree), 20ft (6m) high, 15ft (4.5m) wide, has an open canopy and light foliage able to provide filtered light. In early spring pink, white or purple flowers, rather like butterflies, are carried. Prefers well-drained open soils (Zone 10).

Clethra
Lily-of-the-valley tree

Clethra arborea (lily-of-the-valley tree) is a fine tree, providing an effective screen with its low-branching and evergreen foliage. Its name derives from its fragrant pure white flowers similar to those of the lily-of-the-valley (Zone 8).

ABOVE: Arbutus unedo *(Irish strawberry tree)*

Cornus
Cornel

Most dogwoods are deciduous, but *Cornus capitata* (Bentham's cornel), 30ft (9m) high, 20ft (6m) wide, is an exception. It is a small tree, with greyish leaves and creamy yellow bracts followed by enormous strawberry-like fruit attractive to birds and revealing orange flesh as they are pecked away. Tolerates coastal breezes, industrial pollution and a broad range of soils (Zone 7).

Cupressus
Cypress

Many cypresses are too large for small gardens, though some provide effective hedges, but the fastigiate form of *Cupressus sempervirens* (Italian cypress), 80ft (24m) high, 10ft (3m) wide, can prove useful as a vertical element in a design (Zone 8).

Eucalyptus
Gum

Eucalypts are extraordinarily diverse. Most grow too large for small gardens. Their trunk beauty and remarkable foliage, frequently different in juvenile and mature forms, make them creators of effective and interesting shadow patterns.

Eucalyptus pauciflora (cabbage gum) and *E. niphophila* (snow gum), 20ft (6m) high, 10ft (3m) wide, have attractive bark and foliage and tolerate a wide soil range. Loveliest in flower is *E. ficifolia* (red-flowering gum), 30ft (9m) high, 15ft (4.5m) wide, but it enjoys well-drained soils (Zone 7), while *E. citriodora* (lemon-scented gum), 50ft (15m) high, 20ft (6m) wide, has lovely white bark and lemon leaf scent (Zone 8).

Genista
Broom

Most brooms are shrubs, but *Genista aetnensis* (Mount Etna broom), 15ft (4.5m) high, 10ft (3m) wide, is a small tree with sparse, pendulous, bright green foliage. It casts little shade and can be useful in shrub planting. In late summer its branches cascade with yellow pea flowers. A delightful specimen for open soils (Zone 6).

Gordonia

A small evergreen tree, *Gordonia axillaris*, 20ft (6m) high, 10ft (3m) wide, is outstanding for its glossy bright green leaves and large white winter flowers like those of a single camellia, only larger. It flowers through the winter. Not suited to alkaline soils (Zone 7).

Laurus
Bay laurel

Laurus nobilis (bay), 30ft (9m) high, 20ft (6m) wide, is a useful tree because of the culinary value of its leaves and because it branches low and provides a good screen. It can be clipped and is seen as a ball-headed standard or pyramid at the entrance to houses, a role for which its deep green leaves suit it well (Zone 8).

Ligustrum
Privet

Privets tolerate industrial pollution and heavy soils, qualities that have resulted in their extensive use in urban landscapes. The most deserving of cultivation is *Ligustrum lucidum* (shiny-leaved privet), 25ft (7.5m) high, 10ft (3m) wide, with glossy foliage and masses of creamy flowers in late summer. Birds eat the blue-black fruit with enthusiasm and the tree can become a weed (Zone 8).

Magnolia

A beautiful evergreen tree when in flower, bearing large, cup-shaped, creamy flowers to 8in (20cm) across and large, leathery, dark green leaves on a broad pyramidal tree. Best grown as a specimen, *M. grandiflora* can also be grown as a wall-trained specimen (Zone 7).

Michelia

Smaller than *Magnolia grandiflora*, 40ft (12m) high, 20ft (6m) wide, this member of the magnolia family has evergreen leaves, smaller and pointed, and smaller flowers, scented and ranging from white to pale yellow. It is a splendid tree, flowering in very early spring (Zone 8).

Olea
Olive

The grey foliage of the olive, *Olea europea*, 30ft (9m) high, 15ft (4.5m) wide, is especially lovely above a gnarled trunk. A lovely tree for the Mediterranean garden, producing fruit, a vital part of the world's culinary scene (Zone 8).

Pinus
Pine

Many pines grow too large for small gardens. *Pinus bungeana* (lacebark pine), 60ft (18m) high, 40ft (12m) wide, is rarely available in nurseries, but is worth seeking out for its exquisite peeling bark, which when at its best is reminiscent of a plane (Zone 5).

Pittosporum

An interesting group of trees, containing several, highly decorative, evergreen species suitable for the small garden. Many are useful hedges, being tolerant of clipping and producing small neat leaves. Many of these are cultivars of *Pittosporum tenuifolium*, (kohuhu) 30ft (9m) high, 12ft (3.5m) wide, a fine tree with many small leaves and chocolate-purple flowers emitting a honey scent. A fine cut flower, its delicate foliage makes it a valuable background plant. 'James Stirling' has smaller leaves, while 'Silver Queen' has a white edge to its leaves (Zone 8).

Pittosporum undulatum (sweet pittosporum), 30ft (9m) high, 15ft (4.5m) wide, is a highly desirable ornamental tree with sweetly scented, creamy white flowers and decorative orange fruit. It is wind tolerant and makes an effective coastal windbreak (Zone 8).

Ulmus
Elm

Elms have been lost to disease in recent years, but are now being planted again. Few are lovelier than *Ulmus parvifolia* (Chinese elm), 60ft (18m) high, 40ft (12m) wide, with small leaves and elegant pendulous branches. Its trunk is patterned rust brown flakes and casts a light shade. It can be evergreen though as conditions become colder it tends to lose its leaves in mid-winter (Zone 6).

TEXTURAL PLANTS

Plant textures in small gardens are vital. They permit the development of strong year-round interest and when considered in the context of the built environment they permit contrasts between construction materials and the organic form of leaves. Closer to sitting areas, detail of textures can be especially valuable: cobbles can be used with emergent grasses, or a smooth sculpture clothed in richly textured climbing plants. Careful planning at this level can produce delightful effects, to be sustained through the year. In climates of winter cold, views of such plantings from a house window can be particularly rewarding.

CLIMBERS

Climbing plants offer particular opportunities for textural contrast against walls, through the backs of seats or over a door. There are many fine climbers, though not all offer textural effects. The following offer attraction as interesting textures suited to different uses.

Clematis

There are many excellent clematis, but few possess outstanding foliage. The evergreen *Clematis armandii,* to 18ft (5.5m), though, is effective on a sunny wall, especially trained high and left to tumble. Its leaves are trifoliate and glossy green, bronze on new growth, a fine foil for clusters of pink or white spring flowers (Zone 8).

C. cirrhosa var. *balearica,* to 12ft (3.5m), is delicate with finely divided foliage. Dark green summer foliage becomes bronzy in winter, when it is a perfect foil for the pendulous creamy flowers with internal spots of reddish purple. It is good through a tree or alternatively on an open lattice (Zone 7).

Ficus
Climbing fig

Ficus pumila is an effective self-climbing plant needing to be maintained tightly against a wall to prevent formation of larger, leathery mature leaves. At its best when a tracery of light foliage spreads over a wall—then it appears extremely delicate. It tolerates quite deep shade and dry soil. A form called 'Minima' has an especially small and neat leaf (Zone 8).

Hedera
Ivy

There are many good leaf forms of ivy. Assess those available and make your selection accordingly. One species, *Hedera colchica*, stands out when considering textures. It produces large glossy leaves up to 10in (25cm) across, hanging from the plant in a loose but dramatic way. The variegated 'Dentata Variegata' is very good, as is the distinctly greeny yellow 'Sulphur Heart' (Zone 7).

Hydrangea

Hydrangea anomala subspp. *petiolaris,* to 40ft (12m), is a self-clinging, deciduous climber with neat, heart-shaped, dark lustrous green leaves and peeling dark brown bark. Corymbs of creamy white flowers clothe the plant densely in summer. A fine plant for shaded walls with a rich soil (Zone 5).

ABOVE: The combined textures of Helleborus corsicus *and* Cotinus coggygria 'Notcutt's Variety' *shows how effective even a simple plant massing of foliage can be.*

Parthenocissus

Virginia creeper and Boston ivy are well-enough known. Self-clinging, their foliage dresses the facade of many buildings, adding a splendid character especially rich in fall (autumn). The choicest is *Parthenocissus henryana,* a plant with outstanding foliage of three to five leaflets to each leaf, variegated along the veins with silver and red. Framed against a wall, this is a glorious plant with red fall (autumn) leaves (Zone 5).

Vitis

Vitis coignetiae is one of the finest textured of the climbing plants, producing large, long leaves, up to 10in (25cm) wide and 1ft (30cm) long, but more normally 4in by 8in (10 cm by 20cm), rough on the surface and heart-shaped. Beneath, they bear a rusty brown felt. In fall (autumn), the leaves turn every hue from scarlet through gold, orange, and mahogany (Zone 5).

SHRUBS

Aralia
Japanese angelica tree

Few plants offer more dramatic foliage than *Aralia elata* (Japanese angelica tree), 12ft (3.5m) high, 8ft (2.5m) wide, but it possesses barbarous stem prickles. The large leaves look best against the sky, where their layered effect is at its strongest. This decid-uous shrub has a suckering habit and may be obtained as a variegated form (Zone 7).

Euphorbia

Euphorbia chariacas ssp. *wulfenii*, 4ft (1.2m) high, 3ft (90cm) wide, and *E. mellifera,* 10ft (3m) high, 5ft (1.5m) wide, are both shrubby. The former has evergreen dark grey leaves and large sulphur-yellow flower masses, offering a dramatic spring effect (Zone 7). *E. mellifera* produces mounds of

linear leaves with reddish chocolate spring flower masses (Zone 8). Both prefer sun and good drainage.

Fatsia
Japanese aralia

Fatsia japonica (Japanese aralia), 12ft (3.5m) high, 8ft (2.5m) wide, is enormously shade tolerant and suits a wide range of soil types. It is especially useful in shaded, narrow gardens, where it unfailingly produces its glossy palmate leaves. Its fall (autumn) flower heads are creamy white and are followed by pea-shaped black fruits (Zone 7).

Hebe
Shrubby veronica

There are several excellent hebes, many with rich textures. *Hebe rakaiensis,* 3ft (90cm) high, 4ft (1.2m) wide, has fresh glossy leaves, on a mounding shrub which is a perfect foil to paving. It bears white flowers on racemes in mid-summer (Zone 7).

H. pinguifolia, 2ft (60cm) high, 3ft (90cm) wide, is a silvery-leaved species, best in the form 'Pagei', 1ft (30cm) high, 3ft (90cm) wide, with its mat of small leaves and white flower spikes. As with many grey-leaved plants, this is best in full sun and enjoys good drainage (Zone 7).

Hydrangea
Oak-leaf hydrangea

Hydrangea quercifolia (oak-leaf hydrangea), 6ft (1.8m) high, 4ft (1.2m) wide, has boldly sculptured leaves similar to large oak leaves, heads of fertile and unfertile flowers, white ageing purple and wine-red fall (autumn) tints. Few shrubs offer better year-round performance, but they do best with adequate moisture. They tolerate shade (Zone 5).

Mahonia

Few plants excel more than the mahonias for foliage texture. Many have dark green glossy leaves of magnificent form, and all are evergreen. *Mahonia lomariifolia,* 15ft (4.5m) high, 5ft (1.5m) wide, is an extraordinarily dignified plant at its best when backlit: then the full structure and elegance of the plant becomes apparent. Its foliage texture is quite exceptional, and it produces erect candles of yellow flowers, followed by clusters of blue-black grapes (Zone 8).

It is a parent of *M.* 'Charity', 10ft (3m) high, 8ft (2.5m) wide, a stately shrub producing yellow flowers in long racemes in mid-winter. Both of these plants have a good ability to tolerate shade (Zone 7).

Sorbaria aitchisonii

An elegant shrub with red stems and pinnate leaves, carrying numerous leaflets. Produces masses of creamy white summer flowers, but performs best cut hard back to ground level in spring, when it produces more elegant stems with larger leaves (Zone 6).

Viburnum

Viburnum davidii, 3ft (90cm) high and wide, is a handsome shrub, perfect for falling across the edge of a paved area or a flight of steps. Its beauty lies in its leathery elliptical leaves, a fine foil to paving textures. Uninteresting white flowers are followed by metallic blue berries when male and female forms are grown together (Zone 8).

Yucca

Yuccas are unmistakable with their narrow spiky leaves in clumps. They are useful for their textural quality, providing the ideal focus plant used as a single specimen, but look equally well as a textural mass. *Yucca filimentosa* (Adam's needle), 6ft (1.8m) high, is most effective with fine curling threads along the leaf margin and showy creamy white spikes of pendulous flowers (Zone 6). Yuccas enjoy a sunny well-drained position, none more so than *Y. whipplei* (Our Lord's candle), with slender glaucous leaves and fragrant pendant flowers. Given sufficient sun and good drainage it is the choice among a fine genus (Zone 9).

TEXTURAL GROUND-COVERS

Alchemilla
Lady's mantle

Alchemilla mollis (Lady's mantle), 1ft (30cm) high, 2ft (60cm) wide, provides dense ground-cover, lovely after rain when droplets are held on the leaf hairs to form light diamonds. Acid-yellow flower in summer looks especially good against purple foliages, as in *Cotinus coggygria* 'Atropurpurea'. Grows in sun and light shade and tolerates dryness (Zone 6).

Bergenia
Saxifrage

The bold round leaves of the bergenia are a perfect foil for masonry and paths and provide a low-maintenance border, but not in deep shade. Several species and cultivars are widely available. *Bergenia ciliata*, to 1ft (30cm), has deciduous leaves up to 1ft (30cm) across and bristly, reddish in fall (autumn), and pale pink summer flowers (Zone 7). *B. cordifolia*, to 1ft (30cm), is evergreen, produces pink flowers in spring and is tolerant of a wide temperature range (Zone 5). 'Ballawley', to 9in (23cm), is a hybrid, producing fewer flowers but effective bronze winter foliage (Zone 6). All tolerate a range of soil types but not waterlogging.

Epimedium

A fine group of plants for ground-cover in shade or semi-shade, or in heavy or sandy

soils. The evergreen species and hybrids are especially effective as massed plants beneath shrubs and as a foil to paving. Among the best are the evergreen *Epimedium perralderianum*, to 18in (45cm), tolerant of sun and dryness (Zone 7), the hybrid *E. x rubrum*, to 1ft (30cm), with red young and old foliage, best in shade (Zone 7), and *E. x versicolor*, to 18in (45cm), deciduous and best in the cultivar 'Sulphureum', which flourishes in light shade (Zone 6).

Geranium
Cranesbill

This is a family of superb garden plants of considerable size range. Many possess remarkable deciduous foliage and do best in light shade, but one of the best foliage forms, *Geranium renardii*, to 10in (25cm), enjoys sun. Greyish, rugose and deep-lobed leaves form a wide-spreading rosette. It tolerates partial shade (Zone 9). *G. platypetalum*, to 18in (45cm), is taller and produces vivid, violet-blue flowers above dark green, rugose leaves (Zone 6). There are many other excellent geraniums.

Euphorbia

These are super foliage plants. *Euphorbia amygdaloides* var. *robbiae*, to 1ft (30cm), is one of the choicest ground-covers, with creeping underground rhizomes leading to spreading patches of rosettes of leaves and lime-green flowers. Excellent in even, dry shade (Zone 7). *E. myrsinites* is too open to control weeds effectively, but its glaucous pointed leaves and acid yellow flowers look fine falling over a wall or in contrast to a gravel (Zone 7).

Hosta

Need shade, but form magnificent clumps of deciduous, textured, attractively tinted foliage. There are so many to choose from.

ABOVE: Massings of hosta, saxifrage and ferns show how ground-covers can provide simple but effective cover and also can offer a three-dimensional quality to a planting by extending through a planting scheme.

Hosta plantaginea, to 20in (50cm), produces bright yellow-green leaves and scented white summer flowers. It is the most tolerant of sun (Zone 4). Round bluish-green leaves with strong veins are produced by *Hosta* 'Elegans', to 20in (50cm), which also has white flowers. Best in light shade (Zone 4). There are several variegated forms. 'Thomas Hogg', to 15in (37cm), produces yellow-green leaves with a variable creamy margin, and tall lilac flowers (Zone 4). New cultivars are being introduced. Investigate, and select those best for you.

Limonium
Sea lavender

The texture of foliage and flowers make sea lavenders fine plants for sun. *Limonium latifolium,* up to 1ft (30cm), produces broad leathery, dull green, deciduous leaves and 18in (45cm) masses of lavender-blue flowers (Zone 6). Excellent drought tolerance.

Liriope
Turf lily

This is a tough plant for dry, sunny positions, and will also grow in shade. *Liriope muscari,* to 1ft (30cm), forms steadily increasing clumps with mauve flower spikes in late summer above dark green, grassy evergreen foliage. Effective in extensive masses (Zone 8). *L. spicata*, up to 10in (25cm), is similar in foliage but forms an effective spreader (Zone 6).

Ophiopogon
Mondo grass, turf lily

Evergreen, dark green grassy leaves, attractive small flowers, and blue seeds make this a fine genus of plants. *Ophiopogon japonicus,* to 9in (23cm), is a superb extensive grass-like carpet in sun or part shade (Zone 6). *O. jaburan,* to 1ft (30cm), has larger, broader leaves and very dramatic heads of blue berries (Zone 7) and *O. planiscapus* has intermediate leaves and is best in the blackish-leaved form 'Nigrescens' (Zone 6).

Pachysandra

These are superb evergreen foliage shrubs. *Pachysandra axillaris,* to 9in (23cm), has glossy, broad foliage, and scented white flowers in spring (Zone 5). It is less spreading than *P. terminalis,* to 10in (25cm), with dense-toothed, dark green foliage (Zone 5). Both very shade-tolerant.

EMERGENTS

Dierama
Fairy fishing rods

Clump-forming *Dierama pulcherrimum* has long, grassy evergreen leaves to 40in (110cm), which look especially good emerging from lavenders. It produces pendulous bell flowers of variable shades, from white through pink to pinky mauve on wirey stems. Long-lived, but dislikes root disturbance and dryness (Zone 6).

Dietes
African Iris

These are clump-forming perennials, with grass-like evergreen foliage to 30in (75cm). They are very drought-tolerant, long-lived, and tolerant of a wide range of soil types, even growing in some shade. The white flowers are marked with blue and yellow on *Dietes grandiflora* (Zone 9), while *D. irioides* has cream petals with brown basal markings.

Helichtotrichon
Blue oat grass

Deservedly popular, grey-leaved grass with leaves to 30in (75cm) and flowering stems to 48in (120cm), *Helichtotrichon sempervirens* performs best in good sun and with effective drainage (Zone 4).

Hemerocallis
Day lily

Very popular and deservedly so, these are tough clump-forming plants tolerant of sun and semi-shade but not total dryness. Their massed grassy leaves are fresh green, evergreen in warmer climes, and grow sufficiently densely to block weeds. The species forms were originally yellows and oranges, but today there is an extensive array

ABOVE: The round leaves of the bergenia offer ideal ground coverage. The impact can be heightened by the shadows of an emergent such as Phormium tenax.

of cultivars from yellow, through orange, red, and pink. The species like *Hemerocallis minor,* to 25in (63cm), and *H. flava,* to 30in (75cm), retain an elegance sometimes lost in the cultivars (Zone 4).

Iris

Many irises have excellent foliage form and look very good growing out of rounded leaved ground-covers — some of the sedums, for example. *Iris pallida* 'Variegata' has the advantage of vertically striped, yellowish white variegated leaves up to 2ft (60cm) and lovely soft blue flowers on stems to 3ft (90cm). Enjoys sun (Zone 4).

Kniphofia
Torch lily, red hot poker

Some of the larger species of this group are too coarse and leafy for small gardens, but there are many fine evergreen forms with excellent foliage and good flowers. *Kniphofia thomsonii* var. *snowdenii* produces 2ft (60cm) leaves and coral-pink flowers from summer to late fall (autumn) (Zone 6). Where dramatic effect is required, some of the garden cultivars can be excellent in moist soils and full sun, with flower hues through orange, yellow, and green (Zone 4).

Libertia

Libertia formosa is a most elegant evergreen clump-forming plant with deep green leaves to 30in (75cm), and pure white flowers in summer, followed by decorative orange seed pods. *L. ixioides* is similar, but the leaves turn bronze in winter and are notably smaller, to 2ft (60cm) (Zone 4).

Miscanthus

These are elegant grasses of some size. *Miscanthus sinensis* offers excellent garden forms to contrast with dense shrub masses. It grows to 6ft (1.8m), but is wide-spreading and tolerates some dryness. 'Zebrinus' produces variegated leaves with yellow bands, and 'Gracillimus' is especially dainty with its thin leaves (Zone 4).

Pennisetum
Fountain grass

Pennisetum alopecuroides has grassy leaves to 3ft (90cm), producing indigo, bottle brushes of flowers in late summer. Spreads quickly, but is very tough. Generally coarser than *P. orientale,* to 18in (45cm), with mauve-grey flowers (Zone 4).

Phaiophleps

Phaiophleps nigricans, to 2ft (60cm), is especially useful as foliage texture in paving and gravel because though short-lived it seeds around. Silvery green sword-like leaves carry straw yellow flowers (Zone 5).

Stipa

Stipa gigantea produces elegant flowerheads to 6ft (1.8m) above clumps of dense green leaves. Flowers are purple on opening but dry off to gold (Zone 6).

EVERGREEN SHRUBS

Artemisia
Wormwood

Silvery-toned foliages make an excellent foil for other planting. *Artemisia arborescens* (wormwood) is especially useful. Full sun and well-drained soil suit it best, with a regular clip-over to rejuvenate the foliage. Hedges well (Zone 8).

Camellia

These are ideal plants for the small garden with shade, but need acid soils. They have excellent glossy foliage and flower early in the year. *Camellia sasanqua,* 12ft (3.5m) high, 8ft (2.5m) wide, flowers in winter with small tidy leaves and pliable stems, allowing training against fences and walls. Flower shades vary from white through pink to red (Zone 7). *C. japonica,* 20ft (6m) high, 10ft (3m) wide, has very glossy leaves and a wide range of cultivars, in red, pink, and white. Formal flowers look good in pots — for example, 'Mathotiana Alba' (white) and 'Baron Legnay' (Zone 8). *C.* x *williamsii* and *C. reticulata* also contain magnificent flowering shrubs. There are so many cultivars available it is best to assess what is suitable for your circumstances.

Carpenteria

Carpenteria californica can be grown against a wall where winter protection is needed, but it forms a loose shrub, 12ft (3.5m) high, 12ft (3.5m) wide, if grown in free ground. Wall use may be best in very small gardens. Large white flowers in summer; prefers good drainage (Zone 8).

Cistus
Rock rose

The cistuses are abundantly floriferous, evergreen shrubs requiring sun and effective drainage. They hybridize easily and there are numerous forms around. Among the best are *Cistus ladanifer,* 4ft (1.2m) high, 5ft (1.5m) wide, with sticky resinous leaves and white flowers, frequently with purple basal blotches (Zone 7), *C. albidus,* 6ft (1.8m) high, 6ft (1.8m) deep, with rose-pink flowers and a yellow basal blotch (Zone 6), *C.* x *purpureus* 3ft (90cm) high, 4ft (1.2m) wide, reddish purple with a dark red blotch (Zone 8), and smaller *C. salvifolius,* 2ft (60cm) high, 3ft (90cm) wide, with white flowers and a yellow basal spot (Zone 7).

Clerodendrum

The bright blue flowers of *Clerodendrum ugandense,* 15ft (4.5m) high, 6ft (1.8m) wide, remain on the plant throughout the year and are followed by black berries. Cut back to rejuvenate. The foliage, unfortunately, has an unpleasant metallic smell, so the shrub is best at the rear of a planting scheme. Enjoys full sun. (Zone 10).

ABOVE: This beautiful sandstone wall has a soft golden texture; it does not need to be screened, so the espaliered Camellia sasanqua *is the perfect plant here — evergreen, well-textured and neat. It is clipped against strained wires.*

Convolvulus

Convolvulus cneorum, 2ft (60cm) high, 3ft (90cm) wide, is a silver-leaved, white bell-flowered sub-shrub, excellent in a sunny position and open well-drained soils. Good in raised beds or open walls (Zone 8), as is *C. mauretanicus,* a very low blue-bell flower with slightly silver green leaves, ideal for tumbling over low walls (Zone 10).

Corokia

Remarkable for its form, which is like tangled wire mesh, *Corokia cotoneaster,* 8ft (2.5m) high, 5ft (1.5m) wide, produces small leaves and tiny yellow flowers. It is very salt- and wind-tolerant and can be used effectively, especially where its form can be appreciated (Zone 8).

Cotoneaster

A group of very variable shrubs, some of superb form, and with excellent foliage and fruit. Many do well against a wall. *Cotoneaster salicifolius* var. *floccosus,* to 12ft (3.5m), is especially elegant and dramatic when clothed in red berries (Zone 5). *C. horizontalis,* 3ft (90cm) high, 6ft (1.8m) wide, creates a fishbone branch structure and is deciduous but is even then lovely for its branch tracery. Bears red fall (autumn) berries and is especially good between a wall and paving (Zone 3).

Daphne

Many daphne are difficult to grow but others make a valuable contribution, including *Daphne cneorum,* 1ft (30cm) high, an evergreen trailer producing pink flowers at the end of spring (Zone 5). *D. odora,* 3ft (90cm) high, 4ft (1.2m) wide, a splendidly perfumed plant with pink flowers, is effective near a door or window (Zone 5), and *D.* x *neopolitana,* 3ft (90cm) high, 3ft (90cm) wide, has well-scented rose-pink flowers in early summer (Zone 5).

Euryops

With yellow daisy flowers and deeply incised leaves, *Euryops pectinatus,* 4ft (1.2m) high, 4ft (1.2m) wide, is a splendid drought-tolerant and sun-loving plant enjoying open soils (Zone 9).

Itea

Itea ilicifolia, 12ft (3.5m) high, 12ft (3.5m) wide, produces long, elegant flower racemes of greenish white flowers though the latter part of the summer. Leaf is holly-like but soft green. Looks good against a wall, where the pendulous flowers are seen to full effect (Zone 7).

Loropetalum
Fringe flower

Loropetalum chinense, 6ft (1.8m) high, 6ft (1.8m) wide, is an excellent evergreen shrub with oval, dark green leaves and white ragged flowers in spring. Tends to form a low mound and looks excellent hanging over a wall (Zone 7).

Nerium
Oleander

Nerium oleander, 12ft (3.5m) high, 12ft (3.5m) wide, is a poisonous evergreen shrub with long narrow leaves, producing masses of white or pink flowers throughout summer. Needs sun, and is extremely drought-tolerant (Zone 8).

Osmanthus

The osmanthus are grown for their fragrance, as their flowers are generally quite insignificant. *Osmanthus delavayi,* 8ft (2.5m) high, 10ft (3m) wide, has glossy small leaves and, in spring, small white flowers of outstanding fragrance. It will grow in sun or shade, but prefers well-drained soil. Can be effectively clipped (Zone 7). *O. heterophyllus* produces leaves similar to holly, dark green and very glossy. White fragrant flowers in late summer. Can be effectively hedged, but the form 'Purpureus' is most handsome (Zone 7).

Phlomis
Jerusalem sage

Phlomis fruticosa, 5ft (1.5m) high, 6ft (1.8m) wide, is a sun-loving, drought-tolerant shrub producing dull green, wrinkled leaves and bright yellow, lipped flowers. It is especially effective with purple foliage, for example the purple-leaved sage (Zone 7).

Pinus
Pine

Pinus mugo (dwarf mountain pine) is a very variable shrub, but at its best forms a textured, dark green mound well-suited to emerging from a gravel mulch or with heathers (Zone 6). There are a number of cultivars available, including 'Gnom', 6ft (1.8m) high, 6ft (1.8m) wide, and 'Mops', 4ft (1.2m) high, 4ft (1.2m) wide, the latter a slow-growing form (Zone 4). Keep the size of this plant down by nipping out the growth tips.

Raphiolepis

This is a splendid group of plants, tough, tolerant of drought, shade, and coastal salt. It produces attractive flowers and fruit, but the latter is highly poisonous. *Raphiolepis*

umbellata, 4ft (1.2m) high, 4ft (1.2m) wide, has deep green, glossy leaves, white flowers in early spring and large blue-black fruit (Zone 8), while *R. indica* (Indian hawthorn) produces a smaller leaf and flowers in spring and fall (autumn), from pink to white. A number of cultivars are available, including 'Ballerina', low growing to 3ft (90cm), and 'Springtime', to 6ft (1.8m), with good pink flowers (Zone 9).

Rosmarinus
Rosemary

Rosmarinus officinalis (Rosemary), 4ft (1.2m) high, 4ft (1.2m) wide, is a deservedly popular shrub with attractive evergreen linear foliage, blue-lipped flowers, and perhaps most especially a strongly aromatic leaf fragrance. There are several forms, including 'Benenden Blue', with vivid blue flowers, and 'Miss Jessop's Upright', useful for growing in front of walls but not good where the ground is consistently wet. All forms enjoy sun and prosper if there is good drainage. The species makes a fine tight-clipped hedge (Zone 7).

Senecio

There are many weedy senecios but several are of garden value, none more than the grey-leaved *Senecio* 'Sunshine', 4ft (1.2m) high, 6ft (1.8m) wide, a mound-forming plant, at its best when spilling over the edge of paving. Daisy-like bright yellow flowers are borne throughout the summer (Zone 6).

Skimmia

This is a shade-tolerant group of plants preferring organic rich moist soils but very effective in suitable town gardens, where the mounded plant form, flowers, foliage, and fruit are all attractive. *Skimmia japonica,* 4ft (1.2m) high, 4ft (1.2m) wide, produces

white flowers and bright red berries where male and female plants are grown together. The cultivar 'Rubella', 4ft (1.2m) high, 4ft (1.2m) wide, is a male clone with notably red upper leaves and pink in the bud. *S. reevesiana,* 2ft (60cm) high, 2ft (60cm) wide, produces rich crimson fruit on all plants (Zone 7).

Teucrium

Teucrium fruticans, 8ft (2.5m) high, 6ft (1.8m) wide, produces a twiggy, silver-leaved, blue-flowered shrub, excellent when clipped and best in full sun and with good drainage (Zone 8).

Zauschneria
Californian fuchsia

Zauschneria californica is a small shrub, 3ft (90cm) high, 3ft (90cm) wide, with an excellent ability to tolerate drought. It spreads by rhizomes so can become invasive. Produces grey linear foliage and tubular scarlet flowers (Zone 9).

DECIDUOUS SHRUBS

Berberis

Few shrubs are easier to cultivate than the berberis, tolerating both sun and shade and most soils, except those that are water-logged. Several are evergreen and are very effective, but a number of deciduous species give excellent fall (autumn) foliage hues. All have yellow flowers. Where security in the garden may be important, berberis may be used for their spines. *Berberis thunbergii,* 6ft (1.8m) high, 6ft (1.8m) wide, has fresh green spring foliage, turning red in fall (autumn), with bright red berries. 'Atropurpurea' has striking purple foliage, and 'Aurea' is a dwarf golden-foliaged form (Zone 5). *B. wilsoniae,*

ABOVE: Magnolia stellata *(Star magnolia)*

4ft (1.2m) high, 4ft (1.2m) wide, is elegant, with excellent fall (autumn) foliage and red berries (Zone 5).

Ceratostigma

Ceratostigma willmottianum, 3ft (90cm) high, is an excellent mass planting subject producing deep blue flowers through the latter part of the summer (Zone 5). It is not dissimilar, though larger than, the sub-shrub *C. plumbaginoides,* to 18in (45cm), which reproduces from a creeping rootstock to form a ground-covering carpet. Its bright blue flowers are displayed against the patchy red fall (autumn) foliage (Zone 5).

Cornus
Dogwood

There are many good tree dogwoods. Others form deciduous shrubs when coppiced (cut back to ground level) to reveal their brightly coloured stems. They are best planted near water, where the hues of the stems may be reflected. *Cornus alba* (red-barked dogwood) is most effective, with bright red stems, 'Kesselringii' with its purple-black stems is also good, while *C. stolonifera* 'Flaviramea' has green shoots. Mass planting achieves the best results. All prefer wet soils (Zone 3).

Corylopsis

Corylopsis are elegant shrubs, welcome for their early spring flowers. Their foliage is similar in shape to a hazel, while flowers are carried in pendulous racemes. *Corylopsis sinensis,* 10ft (3m) high, provides fragrant primrose-yellow flowers in early spring *C. willmottiae,* 10ft (3m) high, is very similar, but is often suffused with purple or reddish purple in the leaf, most notably in 'Spring Purple'. These plants look especially good growing across a window, where their branch structure is most obvious (Zone 5).

Coryopteris

Coryopteris x *clandonensis,* 3ft (90cm) high, 2ft (60cm) wide, is an effective deciduous shrub, best in mass plantings in full sun, with good drainage. Its grey foliage is wrinkled above, and a fine foil for the blue flowers. It is best cut back to ground level in winter. Two selections are 'Ferndown', with darker leaves and darker blue flowers, and 'Kew Blue', with darker blue flowers (Zone 8).

Cotinus
Smoke bush

Where strong purple foliage is needed, *Cotinus coggygria,* 15ft (4.5m) high, 15ft (4.5m) wide, cannot be bettered. It does best on poor soils. Grow *C.c.* 'Royal Purple', with its deep wine-purple leaves turning red in fall (autumn), either against acid yellow or with some of the deep red/plum old-fashioned roses. Tolerates dry soils (Zone 6).

Deutzia

Deutzias are perfect for the small garden because of their size and floriferousness. They are easily cultivated, as long as conditions are not dry. Few are taller than 6ft (1.8m). They produce single and double flowers of white and pink. Especially attractive are *Deutzia gracilis*, to 6ft (1.8m), with white flowers, *D.* x *kalmiiflora,* to 7ft (2m), with pale rose flowers, and *D.* x *rosea* 'Carminea', 3ft (90cm), with pale pink flowers on arching branches (Zone 6).

Exochorda
Pearl bush

These are large deciduous shrubs with their arching branches festooned with pure white flowers, lovely in bud, which look like pearls. *Exochorda* x *macranthus* 'The Bride', 6ft (1.8m) high, 8ft (2.5m) wide, has especially pendulous branches, and *E. giraldii* var. *wilsonii,* to 10ft (3m), is more upright and has the largest flowers. They enjoy both sun and part shade and most moist soils (Zone 6).

Magnolia

Many magnolias are trees, but *Magnolia stellata* is a charming deciduous shrub rarely taller than 12ft (3.5m), and slow-growing. It looks very good if the ground is covered by grape-hyacinth beneath. Flowers are white and fragrant, rose-pink ageing white in 'Rosea', and purplish pink in 'Rubra'. Prefer sun or light shade on acid or neutral soils (Zone 7).

Potentilla
Cinquefoil

Potentilla fruticosa, native to the whole northern hemisphere, grows best in cool, moist places. It grows to 3ft (90cm), producing a range of flower shades from white through yellow to orange and red. Notable cultivars include 'Elizabeth' ('Sutter's Gold' — USA), primrose-yellow; 'Katherine Dykes', canary yellow; 'Tangerine', a soft pale orange; and 'Red Ace'

red, fading in hot, dry weather. Excellent shrubby bush with flowers summer through (Zone 2).

Prunus

Plants of this genus have been discussed under "Trees". However, *Prunus glandulosa,* 4ft (1.2m), is a suckering deciduous shrub, best cut to ground level after flowering in spring. It is grown as a thicket. The pink flowers are effective but better in 'Alba Plena', a double white, and 'Rosea Plena', a double pink. Tolerates dry soils (Zone 6).

Spiraea

This is an elegant group of mostly spring-flowering shrubs, of perfect size for small gardens. Many are quite lovely. *Spiraea* x *arguta* (bridal wreath), to 8ft (2.5m), bears clusters of pure white flowers above arching stems and is outstanding (Zone 6). *S. cantoniensis,* to 6ft (1.8m), has white flowers best in the double form 'Lanceata' (Zone 7). *S. thunbergii,* to 5ft (1.5m), is elegant, the white flowers borne early against the fresh green foliage (Zone 5). *S.* x *bumaldii* 'Anthony Waterer', to 5ft (1.5m), has carmine flowers with foliage frequently variegated pink or white (Zone 5).

Viburnum

Viburnums are outstanding evergreen and deciduous shrubs. *Viburnum opulus* (guelder rose) to 10ft (3m), produces cymes of sterile and fertile flowers followed by branches of glistening, translucent fruits. In 'Xanthocarpum' fruits are orange, yellow in 'Fructuluteo'. *V.* x *juddii,* to 6ft (1.8m), which produces sweetly scented, pink flowers in early summer.

CLIMBERS AND WALL SHRUBS
Actinidia

Actinidia chinensis (Chinese gooseberry or kiwi fruit) is very vigorous, to 30ft (9m), with large hairy leaves. Sun or shade and any soil suits this plant. Male and female plants are required for fruit production (Zone 7). *A. kolomikta* is less vigorous, to 12ft (3.5m), with pretty leaves, the lower half washed cream with pink suffusion. These develop best in sun, though the plant tolerates shade (Zone 5).

Akebia

Twining stems ensure *Akebia quinata* gains an effective hold on pergolas, bowers, and fences. It grows to 30ft (9m) and may need to be controlled; otherwise, tidy up old leaves. Leaves are divided into pretty, small leaflets, and the female flowers rich chocolate-purple, the male pale purple and much smaller (Zone 7).

Bougainvillea

This evergreen vine gives a really tropical effect to the garden. Bright and dramatic, *Bougainvillea spectabilis,* to 30ft (9m), has cultivars producing enchanting bracts of purple, red, pink, bronze, and white. Needs little water and lots of sun and can even tolerate light frost (Zone 10).

Ceanothus
Californian lilac

These handsome shrubs can be grown in the open ground, but they make excellent wall plants too for a sunny wall, this approach helping to counter the lax habit of some of these plants. *Ceanothus thyrsiflorus,* to 15ft (4.5m), has bright blue, early summer flowers, *C.* 'Gloire de Versailles', to 12ft

ABOVE: Gelsemium sempervirens (*Carolina jasmine*)

(3.5m), is deciduous and produces powder blue flowers in late summer, while 'A.T. Johnson' produces rich blue flowers n spring and fall (autumn). This is a selection only from among the many excellent plants in this group. Good drainage essential.

Clematis

This is a family of outstanding climbers well-suited to the small garden for their size and fine flowers. Clematis are enormously variable in flower hue and size. Some choice forms include *Clematis florida* 'Sieboldii', not vigorous, to 8ft (2.5m), deciduous, producing white flowers with a purple anemone centre in mid-summer (Zone 7); *C.* 'Vyvyan Pennell', to 11ft (3.5m), deciduous, producing deep violet-blue, double flowers in early summer followed by single flowers

in fall (autumn); *C.* 'Etoile Rose', to 12ft (3.5m), deciduous, producing cherry-purple open bell flowers in late summer, (Zone 6); *C. macropetala* 'Markham's Pink', to 12ft (3.5m), deciduous, with flowers of whipped strawberry pink (Zone 5), and *C. paniculata,* to 12ft (3.5m), with evergreen glossy foliage, and male flowers large and white with yellow anthers (Zone 8). Clematis prefer cool roots and growing into the sun.

Euonymus

Euonymus fortunei var. *radicans* is an evergreen self-clinging climber effective on walls if clipped back. There are several excellent forms: 'Silver Queen', to 10ft (3m), green and white variegations; 'Emerald Gaiety', to 6ft (1.8m), green foliage; and 'Variegatus', greyish-green with white margins (Zone 4). Tolerant of range of soils, sun and shade.

Fremontodendron

These are loose evergreen shrubs effective against a wall. *Fremontodendron californicum,* to 20ft (6m), produces cupped golden-yellow flowers through the summer. Open well-drained soils and full sun are required (Zone 8).

Garrya
Tassel tree

Garrya elliptica forms a lax evergreen shrub, to 8ft (2.5m), but displays its pendulous green catkins best if grown against a wall. It will tolerate shade, pollution, and coastal salt, but is best in sun. Select the male form 'James Roof' with longer catkins to 14in (35cm). Prefers an open soil (Zone 7).

Hardenbergia

Hardenbergia is a genus of twining climbers for pergola or lattice. *Hardenbergia violacea,* to 10ft (3m), produces evergreen, leathery leaves and pea flowers, violet, pink, or white in spring (Zone 8). *H. comptoniana,* to 8ft (2.5m), produces blue flowers but needs open soils (Zone 10).

Gelsemium
Carolina jessamine

Gelsemium sempervirens is an evergreen, twining climber good against fences or on lattice. It produces masses of yellow bell flowers throughout the summer (Zone 7).

Jasminum
Jasmine

Several plants in this group are excellent for the small garden, notably for their scented flowers. They prefer sun and a well-drained open soil. *Jasminum polyanthum,* to 20ft (6m), is white-flowered, pink in bud and highly floriferous, evergreen and scented, flowering in early spring (Zone 9). *J.* x *stephanense,* to 20ft (6m), is also vigorous, the flowers fragrant and soft pink in summer (Zone 8). *J. offinale,* to 30ft (9m), is the common white jasmine with its fragrant white flowers late in summer (Zone 7).

Lapageria
Chilean bellflower

A connoisseur's plant, *Lapageria rosea,* to 15ft (4.5m), is beautiful in its rosy crimson-flowered form and exquisite in its white form. Its foliage is leathery and evergreen while the flowers are waxy bells about 3in (7-8cm) long, often with a checked pattern. Requires lime-free soil and root moisture, though I have seen it happy in relatively dry environments with suitable mulch (Zone 7).

Lonicera
Honeysuckle

Honeysuckles are part of every childhood memory, so widely are they grown for their pretty flowers and delightful scent. *Lonicera hildebrandiana* (giant honeysuckle) can fill enormous trees, but with severe pruning can be controlled. Its flowers, to 6in (15cm), start white, but yellow with age, and its foliage is evergreen (Zone 9). *L.* x *tellmaniana,* to 18ft (55m), is a deciduous non-scented hybrid producing wonderful yellow flowers, and bronze in bud (Zone 8). *L.* x *brownii* (scarlet trumpet honeysuckle) is evergreen, with scarlet flowers and orange throat but no scent (Zone 7). There are many other desirable honeysuckles. All must have their roots in shade but look good growing into the sun.

Mandevilla
Chilean jasmine

The delightful white-flowered climber *Mandevilla suaveolens,* to 20ft (6m), is exquisitely scented and extremely floriferous

so that it greatly brightens a wall in late summer (Zone 7). There are many other members of this genus grown, including the showy pink-flowered 'Alice du Pont', to 25ft (7.5m), but they require considerable warmth (Zone 10).

Parthenocissus

Parthenocissus quinquifolia (Virginia creeper) is a tall deciduous climber to 45ft (13.5m), too large for most small gardens, but it can be contained to the size of a building where the plant is self-clinging. It usually has fine lobed leaves and bright red fall (autumn) foliage (Zone 4). *P. tricuspidata* (Boston ivy), to 60ft (18m), has most attractive small heart-shaped leaves, but these give way to three-lobed leaves in maturity. It is commonly planted for its outstanding red fall (autumn) foliage (Zone 5).

Pyracantha
Firethorn

Not climbers, but shrubs well-suited to clipping against a wall. This permits the splendid red, orange, and yellow berries to be fully displayed, a wonderful fall (autumn) and early winter effect. These are evergreen shrubs with small, creamy white flowers, but their berries are excellent. *Pyracantha atalantioides,* to 20ft (6m), produces scarlet berries, and the cultivar 'Flava' yellow berries, while the cultivar 'Orange Glow' has orange berries. Select forms propagated by cuttings, as seedlings are not reliably good in berry production (Zone 6).

Schisandra

Schisandra rubriflora is a charming climber to 20ft (6m), with male and female flowers on separate plants. The scented flowers are deep crimson and most attractive when displayed against a wall (Zone 7).

Solanum
Potato vine

Solanum crispum 'Glasnevin', to 20ft (6m), is the first climber I grew, and handsome it is too, with bluish purple, potato flowers containing a yellow anther cone in summer and fall (autumn). It is excellent on a wall in sun (Zone 4). *S. jasminoides,* to 20ft (6m), is a pale blue flower with a greyish tinge, but it is not as popular as the lovely white-flowered 'Album', an excellent smothering climber for fences where a screen is required (Zone 7).

Sollya

Sollya heterophylla, to 10ft (3m), is a delicate climber requiring well-drained soils and sun to perform well. It produces delicate, pale blue flowers in small clusters. It can be grown on a loose frame but it is also effective scrambling through shrubs (Zone 7).

Trachelospermum

This is a lovely evergreen group of plants, twining their way up lattice and wire. *Trachelospermum asiaticum,* to 20ft (6m), has neat growth and glossy leaves and numerous white flowers, though it is less scented than *T. jasminoides,* which grows to 30ft (9m), and is a wonderful climber, again with white flowers. Both are very shade tolerant and useful where shaded fences should be screened (Zone 7).

GROUND-COVERS

Ajuga
Bugle

This is an obliging group of ground-covers, their leaves hugging the ground to give an effective cover. *Ajuga reptans* (bugle) , throws up blue flower spikes to about 6in (15cm). There are various leaf forms and variations.

Takes sun or partial shade but scorches in hot, dry situations (Zone 4).

Anthemis

Anthemis cuppaniana is a delightful silver-leaved ground-cover with large daisy flowers reaching 15in (37cm). Though it is always prescribed for sun, in my experience it tolerates significant shade, one of the few silver foliage plants to do so. Clip back to prevent legginess (Zone 8). *A. nobilis* (chamomile), to 5in (13cm), is often recommended for use as a lawn alternative on sandy soil in full sun, but it needs work since it is rarely sufficiently dense to combat weeds (Zone 8). *A. tinctoria,* to 15in (37cm), is a useful cover for the front of borders, best in the outstanding 'E. C. Buxton' with its pale yellow petals (Zone 6).

Campanula
Bell flower

These are excellent flowering plants, preferring sun, or, at the most, light shade. *Campanula carpatica* (Zone 4), to 9in (23cm), produces dense foliage and masses of up-turned flowers in shades of blue. *C. poscharskyana* (Zone 4), to 9in (23cm), is invasive, and can swamp adjacent plants if not controlled, but its lavender-blue star flowers are lovely while *C. portenschlagiana*, to 8in (20cm), is less invasive but almost as effective (Zone 5).

Erigeron

Mexican daisy *Erigeron mucronatus* is a joyous little plant, to 18in (45cm), with masses of loose foliage and daisy-like flowers, pink in bud. It can become invasive and a nuisance if not controlled. Prefers sun and good drainage. Cut back hard after flowering to maintain density and tightness (Zone 8).

Helianthemum
Rock rose

Where full sun is available, these make unbeatable ground-covers, covered as they are with masses of delicate flowers from white through yellow, orange, pink, and red, depending upon the form selected. They are forms of *Helianthemum nummularium,* itself a bright yellow. Needs good drainage and a clipping-over to prevent legginess (Zone 6).

Hypericum

Hypericum calycinum is a most reliable ground-cover to 1ft (30cm), with light green foliage and a succession of bright yellow summer flowers, growing in sun or shade. It will tolerate dry conditions but can be invasive. Best if clipped-over to rejuvenate annually (Zone 6). *H. olympicum,* to 9in (23cm), is more delicate, but not as effective as a weed suppressant. Needs full sun and good drainage and produces bright yellow summer flowers, pale yellow in 'Sulphureum' (Zone 8).

Iris

Most irises lack the foliage density to be an effective ground-cover, if effectiveness includes combating weeds. However, *Iris unguicularis* produces masses of grass-like foliage in clumps to 15in (35cm), sufficiently dense to shade weeds. Be careful not to feed too much nitrogen, or the results could be overwhelming. Delicate iris flowers in shades from dark blue to white are produced deep in the foliage from winter to early spring. Cut this back in late fall (autumn) to reveal the flowers fully where they are sitting above the foliage (Zone 6).

ABOVE: Anthemis tinctoria *'E.C. Buxton'*

Lamium

Lamium galeobdelon (yellow archangel), to 1ft (30cm), is too vigorous for small gardens except as a carpet beneath a tree, but the neat *L. maculatum* has considerable merit. Growing to 8in (20cm), most forms have striking foliage patterns: 'Aureum' has yellow foliage, 'Silbergroschen' has white leaves, and 'Album' has white flowers and silver foliage flash. Especially useful for shade and heavy soils (Zone 6).

Nepeta
Catmint

For ground-cover at the edge of plantings of lavenders or roses, *Nepeta* x *faasenii* (catmint) takes a lot of beating. With pungent silvery foliage to 10in (25cm), and massed soft mauve flowers to 18in (45cm), this ground-cover falls over path edges to provide a delightful softness. Sun, open soils, and a heavy cutting back at the end of the season are vital (Zone 6).

Omphalodes

I have always enjoyed *Omphalodes cappodocica,* to 8in (20cm), and *O. verna,* to 4in (10cm), two self-effacing but obliging ground-covers with delicate blue flowers, more numerous in the former type, which is a little more showy. *O. cappodocica* flowers from spring to early summer above mounded, fresh green foliage in sun or part shade, while *O. verna* flowers at a similar time but is more shade tolerant (Zone 7 *O. cappadocica,* Zone 5 *O. verna*).

Osteospermum

Osteospermum fruticosum is a quick cover for sunny locations and is especially useful where cover is needed on a sunny slope. It grows 1ft (30cm) tall, and is evergreen, with daisy flowers opening lilac and with age becoming white with purple in the middle (Zone 8).

Saxifraga

Many of this group are not sufficiently robust for massed ground-cover effects, though there are several that provide effective and attractive cover. *Saxifraga stolonifera,* up to 5in (13cm), bears roundish evergreen leaves beautifuly marbled with grey and cream and a delicate haze of small white flowers up to 1ft (30cm). It can be a most effective cover in shade, carpeting the ground densely (Zone 8). *S.* x *urbium,* 'London Pride', is especially attractive at the base of tubs, etc. (Zone 7).

Stachys

In full sun, the woolly silver leaves of *Stachys byzantina* 'Lamb's Ears', to 4in (10cm), offer one of the most effective ground-covers. They can look bedraggled if consistently wet. They are at their best in a hot, dry, sunny location, where they will form a carpet. Tall flower spikes to 20in (50cm) are produced, woolly and with small mauve flowers. 'Silver Carpet' is a non-flowering form while 'Primrose Heron' has yellow leaves, but not the style of the silver foliage forms (Zone 6).

Tiarella

Tiarella cordifolia, to 4in (10cm), is a fine ground-cover for moist shade, throwing up creamy white feathery spikes of flowers above lobed leaves, bronzing in winter (Zone 6). *T. wherryi* is more delicate in flower and a tremendous plant for cool shade, but not as prolific and spreading as *T. cordifolia.* It is larger, foliage to 5in (15cm), flowers on long spikes to 15in (35cm), and often pinkish (Zone 6).

Waldsteinia

The dark, lobed leaves of *Waldsteinia* are a little like those of a buttercup. Growing to a height of 4in (10cm), they are a fine foil for the bright yellow flowers in early summer. Performs well in shade and semi-shade but best if not dry (Zone 6).

HERBACEOUS PERENNIALS

Achillea

Achillea are good in full sun. The bright yellow flower forms are especially good combined with blues, such as the dwarf forms of agapanthus or blue sages. *Achillea* 'Moonshine', to 2ft (60cm), is bright light yellow above grey-green feathery foliage. 'Coronation Gold', to 3ft (90cm), has yellow flowers and grey foliage, while *A. filipendulina* 'Gold Plate' is taller still, to 4ft (1.2m) (Zone 5).

Anemone

The different forms of *Anemone* x *hybrida* are quite confused, but they are lovely, flowering in late summer, when their attractive hue is very welcome. *A.* 'Honorine Jobert' is a lovely white, 'Hybrida' is pale pink, both may grow to 3ft (90cm) in flower. Invasive especially where there is sufficient moisture; however, will tolerate shade well (Zone 6).

Arthropodium
Rock lily

Arthropodium cirrhatum is a lovely plant, growing in sun but surprisingly tolerant of shade and coastal salt. The leaves are strap-like and grey-green, while the white flowers are very waxy, with mauve and orange central pointels, and quite beautiful. Superb in masses and dead easy from seed (Zone 8).

ABOVE: Helleborus orientalis *(Lenten rose)*

Coreopsis

Coreopsis verticillata, to 2ft (60cm), is an outstanding garden plant with fine foliage and repeat yellow flowers for sunny gardens. There are many forms in various yellows (Zone 5).

Corydalis

One of the few plants that has grown in all my gardens, *Corydalis ochroleuca* forms 1ft (30cm) clumps of fern-like grey foliage with creamy white flowers above. It seeds into niches in paving and walls, where it looks beautiful. Drought-tolerant (Zone 7).

Echinacea

Echinacea purpurea, to 4ft (1.2m), is a stout-stemmed perennial with rather coarse leaves performing well in sun and most soils. It looks superb with silver foliage plants and light mauves, for example soft-tinted Sidalceas. There are several cultivars, including a white-flowered form (Zone 6).

Erysimum

Late winter brings out the intense hues of the erysimum flowers that brighten the shade-edge of mature gardens. The mauve-flowered *Erysimum* 'Bowles Mauve', to 3ft (90cm), forms a splendid mound, the silvery green foliage providing a most effective foil for the flowers, which continue for a prolonged period from late winter. It enjoys sun and semi-shade, even on poor soils (Zone 6). 'Constant Cheer' produces flowers of a browny orange ageing purple, while 'Bredon' has reddish buds and bright orange flowers. Fine plants to let fall across gravel paving.

Gaura

The extended flowering period of *Gaura lindheimeri,* to 3ft (90cm), makes it a most

Campanula

An excellent group of plants, many of them ideal for mixing with roses and as part of a bright and traditional gardening approach. *Campanula alliarifolia,* to 3ft (90cm), forms clumps of heart-shaped foliage above which are carried cream bells on long stems in summer. A most elegant plant for sun and shade where there is soil moisture (Zone 6). *C. lactiflora,* to 4ft (1.2m), forms large clumps, well-suited to mixing with open shrubs which give the plants support. Flowers in lilacs, soft blue, and white (Zone 5). *C. latiloba,* to 3ft (90cm), forms rosettes of foliage, which offer good ground-cover and also produce wide, cup-shaped rich lavender-blue flowers. There is a good white form (Zone 6). It is not greatly different from *C. persicifolia*, which has fewer open flowers and thinner stems. The white form is excellent (Zone 5).

Centranthus
Valerian

Centranthus ruber, to 3ft (90cm), provides a most effective massed plant naturalizing in retaining walls and paving areas. The foliage is glaucous, while masses of pink flowers are produced in spring above this. They are long-lasting and very informal. A white-flowered form is excellent. Best where drainage is good (Zone 6).

usable plant, especially beneath tea roses, where it provides a cover for the unattractive woodiness of their trunks. Its foliage is undramatic but produces long wands of white and pink flowers like delicate small butterflies. Cut this plant back hard in mid-summer to prevent excessive legginess and encourage a second period of flowering. Enjoys sun and is drought-tolerant (Zone 5).

Geranium
Cranesbill

This is an outstanding group of plants for foliage and flowers, most notable for their ability to tolerate even quite deep shade. Selecting from them is difficult. *Geranium endressii,* to 18in (45cm), is especially handsome, with divided leaves and chalky pink flowers through summer. 'Wargrave Pink' is similar but with denser foliage to 2ft (60cm) and masses of small pink flowers (Zone 6). 'Johnson's Blue', to 1ft (30cm), is an excellent massing plant producing prolific lavender-blue flowers over deeply divided foliage (Zone 5).

Hedychium
Ginger lily

These are large plants, producing dramatic flowers and foliage. *Hedychium gardnerianum,* to 5ft (1.5m), has rhizomes that need to be just covered by mulch and produce stout stalks with deep green leaves best in shade. In late summer, clear yellow flowers with projecting red stamens are produced. Gives a ravishing perfume and makes an excellent cut flower (Zone 9).

Helleborus

These are fine plants with many good qualities. *Helleborus argutifolius* is a quite

outstanding plant with trifoliate stiff leaves, veined and greyish green. Looks especially good against a purple leaf form of *Cotinus coggygria.* Takes some shade (Zone 8). *H. orientalis,* the lenten rose, is very variable. Divide plants to ensure you retain the flower shade you want and seek out pure white and reddish-purple forms. Evergreen foliage is itself attractive and does best in a shaded setting (Zone 7).

Heuchera

These are splendid mound-forming plants, with woody base and foliage so dense that weed growth is precluded. They look especially good when massed. *Heuchera micrantha* forms a mound of foliage to 9in (23cm), with a long wiry stem above bearing bluish white flowers. I prefer the form 'Palace Purple' with blackish purple leaves, a first-rate plant. As with all this group, they prefer fertile soils, but will tolerate a surprising amount of sun (Zone 6). *H. sanguinea,* to 1ft (30cm), produces mats with numerous red flowers to 20in (50cm), which are most striking in selected forms, such as 'Red Spangles' (Zone 5).

Iris

There are many to choose from, and selecting the best is never easy. *Iris foetidissima,* to 18in (45cm), is not the best in flower, being variably yellowish with purplish markings, but the joy comes in fall (autumn), when the seed pods split to reveal masses of orange seeds. It will grow in quite deep shade (Zone 6). *I. japonica,* to 18in (45cm), is another shade-tolerant species with soft, powder blue flowers on branched stems, though there are white and darker blue forms (Zone 7). *I. missouriensis,* to 20in (50cm), is extremely elegant with its foliage and handsome blue flowers, but it must have

wet ground in spring, even if dry later (Zone 7). *I. kerneriana,* to 18in (45cm), has narrow leaves and the most beautifully shaped, soft yellow flowers in mid-summer. Enjoys dry, sunny locations (Zone 7).

Lychnis

Lychnis coronaria is an outstanding plant; however, given too much irrigation and nutrient, it grows lush mounds of foliage. Regular division is recommended. Grown well it produces attractive grey foliage and massed purplish pink flowers, reaching 3ft (90cm). The choice form is the white-flowered 'Alba' (Zone 5).

Lysimachia

Lysimachia clethroides and *L. punctata,* both to 3ft (90cm), can be invasive, yet they are both fine plants. The former produces spikes of white flowers bent over at their top in bud, and straightening as the flowers open (Zone 5). *L. punctata* produces rich yellow flowers especially good against the fresh green foliage. It can be invasive where wet soils exist. It looks especially dramatic with purples — for example, the purple flowers of *Clematis jackmannii* (Zone 6).

Parahebe

The blue of the flowers of *Parahebe perfoliata* is so breathtaking that you feel you have to grow this plant. Flowering in early summer, it is best grown as a sprawler through low shrubs, when with support it will reach 30in (75cm). Best in full sun and well-drained soils (Zone 6).

Penstemon

This group of plants looks especially dramatic with some of the old roses. They enjoy sun and a well-drained soil, most commonly producing flowers from white to pink and red. The pink 'Hidcote Pink', to 30in (75cm), is charming, 'Thorn' has large flowers in white and pink, and 'Burford Purple' is a magenta (Zone 7).

Perovskia
Russian sage

Perovskia atriplicifolia, to 4ft (1.2m), is quite simply an outstanding plant for massing in full sun, with grey-white foliage supporting spires of lavender-blue flowers (Zone 8). A choice form is 'Blue Spire', with more branching stems (Zone 6). Both are really shrubs, but are best cut back to ground level on completion of flowering.

Rudbeckia

These are superb large daisies, some perhaps rather large for the smaller garden. *Rudbeckia laciniata*, for example, reaches 6ft (1.8m), but it is a fine plant with deeply cut leaves and large yellow flowers in summer (Zone 5). *R. fulgida* 'Goldsturn' is an outstanding plant to 2ft (60cm), with yellow-rayed flowers and a black central cone (Zone 5). All require a fertile soil in full sun with reasonable moisture.

Salvia

There are good herbaceous salvias, many of them offering excellent shades. *Salvia nemorosa*, to 3ft (90cm), is usually grown in the form 'Superba', with violet-blue flowers from mid-summer (Zone 6). *S. farinacea*, to 4ft (1.2m), is long-flowering and available in many forms, such as the white-flowered 'Alba' and the glorious deep blue 'Victoria' (Zone 7).

Sedum

This is a group of rather succulent foliage plants, producing massed flowerheads.

Sedum aizoon 'Aurantiacum', 18in (45cm), flowers in summer, producing masses of bright yellow flowers above broad dark leaves. Stems and seed capsules are deep red (Zone 5). *S. spectabile*, to 18in (45cm), is the choice for the garden, notably in the forms 'Carmen', mauve-pink, or 'Autumn Joy', with its rich pink flat heads becoming coppery red as they age. The leaves form clumps of grey-green foliage, best divided as they become larger (Zone 6). 'Autumn Joy' is best in large blocks and attracts butterflies.

Sidalcea

Sidalcea malviflora, to 3ft (90cm), produces clumps of basal foliage from which grows a flowering spike like a small hollyhock, very delicate and very pretty. There are a number of cultivars. 'Rose Queen', with soft pink flowers, is one of the loveliest. *S. candida*, to 40in (1.3m), provides white flowers, though these are quite small. Requires sun (Zone 6).

Viola
Violet

This is one of the most popular garden plants. *Viola cornuta*, to 1ft (30cm), is larger than many of the more delicate species, but a desirable plant as a shade ground-cover, with forms providing flower shades from white through blues to violet (Zone 5).

Zantedeschia
Arum lily

Zantadeschia aethiopica (arum lily), to 4ft (1.2m), is a plant with enormous presence both in its dark green leaves and its white spathes and yellow spadices. It requires moisture, and with this available will perform as an evergreen in warm climates, though as colder conditions occur it becomes deciduous, needing winter protection where frosts occur.

BULBS

Arum

Arum italicum is a handsome plant, producing deep green hastate leaves in fall (autumn). The great quality of these leaves lies in their rich surface marbling. Flowers of a spathe are produced in spring, though likely to go almost unnoticed. The leaves die down through summer and the next thing seen is the head of bright orange fruit. Hardly a better cover for dry shade (Zone 5).

Clivia

Two species of these plants are cultivated in gardens. *Clivia miniata* and *C. nobilis*, both of outstanding quality for their evergreen foliage which is strap-like and handsome, are able to grow in extreme shade; indeed, their leaves scorch in sun. *C. miniata*, up to 20in (50cm), varies in tone from orange-scarlet through orange to yellow, with upward-facing flowers, while *C. nobilis*, similar in size, produces hanging orange flowers (Zone 10).

Cyclamen

For general garden use, two species are quite outstanding. *Cyclamen hederifolium* flowers in fall (autumn), with a mass display of its lilac-pink flowers, the leaves developing after the flowers. The foliage is not large, and is variable in shape, with silver and grey surface markings making the leaves extremely beautiful once established. This is a very tough plant for cultivation beneath deciduous or evergreen trees, and will even grow in grasses. *C. coum* is a late winter- and spring-flowering species with far more rounded leaves and pink flowers on shorter stems than *C. hederifolium* (Zone 5).

Fritillaria

Fritillaria imperialis is a plant with real poise. It has pendulous orange bells, to 4ft (1.2m), produced in spring, with elegant, leaf-like bracts above. There is a yellow-flowered form 'Lutea', of even greater beauty (Zone 6).

Narcissus
Daffodil

Many of these plants naturalize superbly well, and though space in the small garden may be such that they can only be grown in limited numbers, they are a welcome addition to any garden. Where space is restricted, some of the smaller species are especially welcome, such as *Narcissus bulbocodium,* to 6in (15cm), which varies in flower hue from pale lemon yellow to golden. Among cultivar forms, 'February Gold', to 15in (35cm), with gold petals and darker trumpets, and 'Jack Snipe', to 1ft (30cm), with white flowers and lemon-yellow trumpets, are most suitable (Zone 5).

Nerine

These are lovely bulbs, ideal for mass planting in sun or light shade. The more delicate forms, for example the 1ft (30cm) *Nerine filifolia*, with its pale pink flowers, are quite a contrast to more robust species like *N. sarniensis,* to 25in (63cm). *N. bowdenii* is another robust species to 25in (63cm), with white and pink forms (Zone 7).

Tulbaghia
Society garlic

This is an evergreen, bulbous-rooted perennial. *Tulbaghia violacea,* to 1ft (30cm), produces narrow blue-grey leaves and lilac-purple flowers, which continue sporadically through the winter. Looks handsome against a background of silver-grey foliage (Zone 7).

ABOVE: Clivia miniata

Tulipa

These are popular flowering bulbs of great grace and elegance, and while there are enormous numbers of cultivars, many of the species are well worth growing. *Tulipa sprengeri,* 10in (25cm), for example, flowers late and produces the most delicate and elegant orange-red flowers. *T. saxatilis,* 10in (25cm), is, in contrast, early in flower, producing pink to lilac flowers with a large yellow internal petal base. The narrow growth of tulips means that they are ideal for interplanting with other plants, especially herbaceous material, through which they can grow and flower before the herbaceous plants.

ROSES

There are so many roses to choose from. Those selected for the small garden need to provide interest for an extended period, and this means they should be recurrent, that is, provide repeat flowering after their first blooms — or they might provide attractive hips. There is also a need, in the small garden, for roses not to be too large. Some of the climbing roses, particularly, can become very large, and controlling them can be quite difficult. It is preferable to select a rose suited to the scale of your garden.

Rosa moyesii

These are elegent roses with fern-like deciduous foliage that makes them especially elegant. The two most frequently cultivated forms are 'Highdownensis', to 10ft (3m), with long arching canes and crimson flowers, producing bottle-shaped hips, and 'Geranium', to 8ft (2.5m), with bright red flowers and large hips. These are best planted to grow over your head or with a delicate climber running through them.

Albas

These are vigorous and tough roses of ancient ancestry. They produce long upright canes, clothed in light green foliage and bearing elegant flowers through spring. Favorites include 'Maiden's Blush', to 7ft (2m), a soft warm pink of great beauty, 'Konigin von Danemark', to 6ft (1.8m), with quartered flowers of a pale rich pink, and 'Félicité Parmentier', to 5ft (1.5m), which opens pink and tight in flower. As this ages, the petals reflex and the flowers change to white. This is one of the few groups of roses that have the ability to perform well in shade.

Gallicas

Gallicas flower only once in the spring, but their value in the small garden lies in their small size and beautifully scented flowers. Though they flower only once, their flowers are charming, and their tolerance to soil type makes them widely grown. 'Cardinal de Richelieu', to 4ft (1.2m), produces lovely dark purple, perfumed flowers, darker than the highly perfumed 'Charles de Mills', with its crimson-purple flowers that fade to reddish purple. 'Duchesse de Montebello', to 5ft (1.5m), is much paler, with pale pink, scented flowers on a lax form and borne against fresh green foliage. Where space permits, 'Duchesse D'Angouleme', to 4ft (1.2m), is a lovely rose, not as tall, but with a spreading habit. It is laden with delicate pale pink, globular flowers.

Portland roses

This group is fragrant, recurrent and small, ideal for the small garden or for growing in pots. Among these are some of the loveliest

roses, including 'Comte de Chambord', to 6ft (1.8m), a purplish pink rose producing a sweetly scented flower, and 'Jacques Cartier', to 4ft (1.2m), softer pink with a pronounced eye and a delightful scent.

Damask roses

Damask roses are robust roses, prolific in flower and long in season. 'Ispahan', to 6ft (1.8m), is one of the first old roses to open and one of the last to finish producing clusters of rich pink flowers on a bushy, rather upright shrub. 'Mme Hardy', to 6ft (1.8m), has been described as "one of the most superlatively beautiful of the old white varieties", and produces white flowers with a green central eye on a plant that is markedly upright in form.

Moss roses

This group of roses have a moss-like growth around their flowers and buds, and this looks wonderful against the rich pinks and plums of their flowers. None reveals these tones better than the wonderfully dark 'Nuits de Young', to 5ft (1.5m), a thin bush, but certainly the darkest of the roses, flowering only in mid-summer. It is fragrant, as is the lovely 'Soupert et Notting', a low bush to 4ft (1.2m) with a pretty pink flower. This is recurrent, as are some others of this group, including 'Mme Louis Lévêque', to 5ft (1.5m), with deep pink flowers and 'Deuil de Paul Fontaine', to 3ft (90cm), with quartered rose to purple flowers.

Bourbons

These roses grow too large for some of the smaller gardens. Indeed, some are so prolific that they are better handled as pillar roses, though winter pruning keeps them to a more convenient shape. Their great qualities are their ability to flower

perpetually and their richly scented flowers. 'La Reine Victoria', to 6ft (1.8m), produces arching branches with most delightful full, rounded flowers of faded pink. From this originated the sport 'Mme. Pierre Oger', to 6ft (1.8m), sparse but producing creamy pink flowers, even better than those of the parent, with a fine scent.

'Souvenir de la Malmaison' is a climber reaching 12ft (3.5m). However, a bush form is available to 3ft (90cm) with the palest pink quartered flowers charmingly and idiosyncratically scented. Sports from this include 'Kronprinzessin Viktoria', to 4ft (1.2m), a creamy yellow-flowered sport of excellent fragrance, and 'Souvenir de St. Anne's', to 7ft (2m), a bushy plant producing almost single pink flowers.

So good are the bourbon roses that there are many other well-known forms also worthy of consideration for small gardens, though many grow quite large.

Hybrid Perpetuals

The Hybrid Perpetual roses were produced by rose breeders in enormous numbers in the last years of the 19th century. They were roses with a recurrent flowering character and strong flower hues and many were not really gardenworthy; however, those that are grown tend to be rather large and may be best against a frame or bower.

'Mrs John Laing', to 6ft (1.8m), bears scented pink flowers, excellent for cutting, and has a strong constitution, allowing it to perform well anywhere. 'Reine des Violettes', 6ft (1.8m) by 5ft (1.5m), may be too large for really small gardens, but it is a graceful and floriferous plant with a most telling scent and quartered parma violet flowers. 'Frau Karl Druschki', to 5ft (1.5m), is the perfect white rose, with erect vigorous growth and white flowers with a lemon flush, but it lacks a scent, so vital in the small garden.

Rosa rugosa

This is one of the most useful rose species, with effective flowers, fruit, and foliage. The foliage is thick and coarse and carried densely on the branches, so that the plant is very effective as a weed suppressant, while the mounded form of the plant also contributes to this quality. In general, this is a salt-tolerant species able to thrive in even the harshest conditions. There are many excellent forms. *Rosa rugosa* 'Alba', to 6ft (1.8m), has large single white flowers with orange-red hips, the earliest of them borne at the same time as the last flowers so they look most dramatic together. 'Frau Dagmar Hastrup', to 4ft (1.2m), is more compact, and bears large, clear pink flowers that are wide-open. The hips are rich crimson. Do be careful about some of the forms, because the orange-red hips can clash with the flowers, as in 'Roserie de l'Hay', to 6ft (1.8m), which bears little fruit, and the rather gaudy 'Scabrosa', to 4ft (1.2m), with rich violet-crimson flowers. I particularly enjoy 'Conrad Ferdinand Meyer', to 8ft (2.5m), with its silvery pink flowers and wonderful scent.

Modern roses

Roses are being released onto the market every year, and often it is best to select from a new rose catalogue to identify that form best suited to your needs. There are, however, several roses with an excellent reputation worthy of considering here — many of quite recent origin.

'Buff Beauty', 6ft (1.8m) by 6ft (1.8m), is really described as a hybrid musk rose. It has an arching branch form and bears double, beautifully shaped rich apricot-yellow flowers of excellent scent. It can be trained against a wall. 'Fruhlingsmorgen', to 6ft (1.8m), is surely one of the loveliest of all flowering shrubs, producing wide-open flowers, pink at the edge and passing to

yellow at the center, and with masses of maroon filaments and anthers. It flowers in spring and summer but has the slight problem of poor foliage. 'Raubritter', to 3ft (90cm), has the same breeder, but it is not for the small garden unless a steep bank needs to be covered, when its 7ft (2m) spread can be useful. It produces clusters of pink, semi-double recurved flowers so that they look like scoops of a rich and creamy strawberry ice-cream. It is a beauty.

Superb new roses in the old tradition are being bred by David Austin, an English breeder, and many of his roses are first-rate for small gardens as they are contained, floriferous and delightfully scented. Many of these are magnificent — 'Constance Spry', to 9ft (2.5m), for example, produces large pink scented flowers, but only in summer; 'Chaucer', to 4ft (1.2m), is a delicate shell-pink with a delicious scent; and 'Graham Thomas', to 6ft (1.8m), is a rich orangey yellow and performs outstandingly well

where there is warmth. This group of roses is among the loveliest for the small garden, many with names from English literature or history such as the 'Mary Rose', 'Yeoman', 'Cymbeline', and 'Cressida'.

Climbing roses

There are so many fine climbing roses from which to select. *Rosa* 'Mme Gregoire Staechlin', to 12ft (3.5m), is first-rate with nodding pink flowers and a scent of sweet peas, but sadly it only flowers once. 'Francis E. Lester', to 4ft (1.2m), is a delicious single flower form, opening pink and fading to white with yellow stamens, quite well-suited to the smaller garden. 'Sombreuil', to 12ft (3.5m), has well-scented, quartered flowers continuously produced until fall (autumn), of a soft, creamy yellow. 'Pompon de Paris', to 9ft (2.5m), is a delightful weak climber, producing tiny pink flowers early which are charming through blue shrubs such as ceanothus.

ABOVE: Hybrid Perpetual 'Mrs John Laing'

Index

Acknowledgments

For Tom Wright who gently engendered a love of horticulture into a generation of Wye College students — with thanks

My office works as a team, and completion of this book would not have been possible without the forbearance and tolerance of Barrie Gallacher, Julieanne Boustead, and Mary Papaioannou, who encourage, inspire, cajole and placate me as required, and Bridget Patrick, the administrator and organizer of the office, who simply despairs. Rosie Houseman of The Rose Arbour deserves thanks for being so consistently helpful and patient when I quiz her about her beloved roses. Lynn Bryan and Deborah Nixon of Lansdowne offered every bit of encouragement needed for this project.

Photography credits

The Garden Picture Library (Ron Sutherland/Duane Paul Design Team), Front Cover; The Garden Picture Library (Jerry Pavia), Back Cover; Peter Baistow, Endpapers; Tania Midgley pp.2-3; The Garden Picture Library (Mayer/Lescanff) p.4; Clive Nichols p.5; Clive Nichols (Designer Sue Berger) p.6; Clive Nichols (Designer Anthony Noel) p.9; The Garden Picture Library (Steven Wooster) pp.10-11; The Garden Picture Library (Ron Sutherland) p.12; Jerry Harpur (Fitzgibben, Designer Christopher Madden) p.14; John Patrick p.15; S.&O. Mathews p.16; Clive Nichols (Designer Anthony Noel) p.17; Jerry Harpur (Sir Hardy Amies) p.18; Tania Midgley p.20; Charles Mann (Van den Bark) p.24; Jerry Harpur (Lady Barbirolli) p.28; Jerry Harpur (Designer Arabella Lennox-Boyd) p 32; Clive Nichols (Designer Anthony Noel) p.36; The Garden Picture Library (Steven Wooster, Designer Jane Fearnley) p. 40; Jerry Harpur (Designer Tim du Val) p.45; The Garden Picture Library (Ron Sutherland, Designer Duane Paul Design) p.48; Peter Baistow p.50; Clive Nichols p.51; Peter Baistow p.54; Jerry Harpur (Designer Geoff Kaye) p.55; Clive Nichols p.58; Tania Midgley p.62; The Garden Picture Library (Henk Dijkman) p.64; Peter Baistow p.66; Clive Nichols (Designer Anthony Noel) p. 67; The Garden Picture Library (Perdereau-Thomas) p. 68-69; Peter Baistow p.70; Jerry Harpur (Lee Wheeler, Designer Christopher Madden) p.73; John Patrick p.74-75; Clive Nichols p.76; John Patrick p. 78; Photos Horticultural p.79; Peter Baistow p. 80; S.&O. Mathews pp.82-83; Charles Mann (Van den Bark) p.84; Insight p.85; The Garden Picture Library p.86; Charles Mann (Sally Robertson) p.87; The Garden Picture Library (J.S. Sira) p.89; S.&O. Mathews p.90; The Garden Picture Library (Roger Hyam) p.92; Jerry Harpur (Stephanie Riley) p.94; Tania Midgley p.95; Charles Mann p.96; Clive Nichols p. 98; John Patrick p.101; Ivy Hansen p.104; John Patrick p.106; John Patrick p.108; John Patrick p.109; John Patrick p.111; Ivy Hansen p.113; Ivy Hansen p.115; Ivy Hansen p.117; Ivy Hansen p.119; Ivy Hansen p.122; Lansdowne Publishing (Richard Hersey) p.124

Note to American readers

ZONE RATINGS

The zone rating refers to the minimum temperature a plant will tolerate.

Zone 1	-50°F	Zone 6	0°F
Zone 2	-40°F	Zone 7	10°F
Zone 3	-30°F	Zone 8	20°F
Zone 4	-20°F	Zone 9	30°F
Zone 5	-10°F	Zone 10	40°F
	Zone 11	above 40°F	

First published in the United Kingdom in 1994 by
ANAYA Publishers Ltd
3rd Floor, Strode House
44-50 Osnaburgh Street
London NW1 3ND

Managing Director: Jane Curry
Production Manager: Sally Stokes
Publishing Manager: Deborah Nixon
Designer: Kathie Baxter-Smith
Illustrator: Valerie Price, Miki Brightmore
Copy Editor: Avril Janks
Picture Researchers: Jane Lewis, Kate Oliver

Formatted in Garamond 3 on Quark Xpress
Printed in Singapore by Kyodo Printing Co. (S'pore) Pte Ltd

British Library Cataloguing-in-Publication data

A CIP record for this book is available from the British Library.

ISBN 1-85470-186-X

Front cover: A small garden can make creative use of architectural features, paving and planting.
Back cover: The formal elegance of a traditional pattern garden.
Endpapers: Colour and containers can provide particular interest in a small garden.
Page 2: The varying textures of foliage provide a classical feel and enduring beauty.
Page 4: With proper planning, a garden can be a peaceful haven from the outside world.
Page 5: The seasonal character of bulbs means that they are perfect for container cultivation.
While tulips are often underplanted they also provide superb formal displays. Tulipa 'Princess Irene'.